In Praise of *Breaking Money Silence*

"Kathleen Burns Kingsbury's informed and insightful wisdom will guide you to articulate your money story, and enjoyably inspire you to achieve personal and financial transformation."

—David Krueger, MD, Executive Mentor Coach and Author,
The Secret Language of Money

"*Breaking Money Silence* provides timeless and practical strategies to help advisors and their clients have deeper, more meaningful discussions about money. Kathleen Burns Kingsbury describes the financial and emotional problems that stem from avoiding honest and direct conversations about money. She doesn't just stop there. She shares essential strategies to engage in more effective conversations with family, friends, and colleagues. I particularly enjoyed the coaching exercise to help me increase the confidence to incorporate them into my practice. The money challenges help me integrate these new skills into my life effortlessly."

—Marguerita Cheng, CFP®, Chief Executive Officer,
Blue Ocean Global Wealth Management

"In Kathleen's latest book she advocates that it's time for breaking money silence. I agree and think speaking up about money can change the world! Kathleen says, 'Taboos are made to be broken.' There is no better time than now! Bravo!"

—Cary Carbonaro, MBA, CFP®, Author, *The Money Queen's Guide:
For Women Who Want to Build Wealth and Banish Fear*

"In *Breaking Money Silence*, Kathleen Burns Kingsbury issues an important call to action and empowers individuals and families with practical tips, tools, and resources designed to unleash the economic power and potential of all."

—Kara Underwood, Managing Director, Head of Field
Talent Management, Morgan Stanley

"*Breaking Money Silence* will change your and your clients' lives. Any advisors who believe they are 'holistic' would benefit from living by the principles covered here. Every chapter includes questions, strategies, and tools that are sensible, effective, thoughtful and broken out for both individuals and their advisors. A must-read for anyone in the financial advice business."

—Heather R. Ettinger, Managing Partner,
Fairport Asset Management

"Kathleen once again shines a much-needed spotlight on a critical financial planning topic. *Breaking Money Silence* is not only a good read, but it provides you, as a financial advisor, with tools to help have more effective conversations with your clients. And then, maybe, you'll have them with your family, too."

—Kate Healy, Managing Director, Marketing,
TD Ameritrade Institutional

"Kathleen Burns Kingsbury gets at the heart of financial issues, dispels misconceptions and provides practical insights that lead to transparent conversations. With her help, we can start to level the playing field for genders and generations to improve overall decision-making."

—Brad Best, CWS®, AIF®, Director of Advisor Education,
Cetera Financial Group

"Kingsbury shines a spotlight on the real price that we all pay from believing these money taboos and keeping quiet about money matters. Many books solely focus on the plight of women, but Kingsbury smartly points out that money silence is an equal opportunity issue that affects both sexes and even financial advisors, whom we mistakenly believe have the highest emotional money IQ of all. Rarely will a book change your life and give you the tools you deserve for a richer life—this is one of those books."

—Stacy Francis, CFP®, CDFA™, CES™, President and CEO,
Francis Financial, Inc. and Founder, Savvy Ladies™

"In her latest book, *Breaking Money Silence*, Kathleen Kingsbury turns the high beam of her expertise as an expert in psychology onto a dark and difficult subject: money. Not only does Kingsbury explore why a subject that preoccupies us all is so darn difficult to talk about, but convinces us that our silence costs us plenty when it comes to our wealth and well-being. Best of all, she shows her readers how to change their money mindset and to practice talking about finance with their families, partners, and advisors in a healthy, productive way. If money is the one remaining conversational taboo in our modern 'tell-all' culture, it won't be for long once Kathleen Kingsbury's book gets the attention it deserves."

—Eleanor Blayney, CFP®, Gender Diversity Advisor to CFP Board Center for
Financial Planning and Author, *Women's Worth*

"Kathleen Burns Kingsbury has written a truly awesome book that takes readers on a journey that is entertaining and enlightening. Read *Breaking Money Silence* and you will find your voice and feel empowered to face important questions about your life's goals and how they relate to your relationship with money. One of the greatest strengths of this work is how it provides the tools to take action, with empathy, strength, and awareness. Brilliant work!"

—Michael F. Kay, CFP®, President, Financial Life Focus

"As a woman who personally knows the high price of money silence, I highly recommend that you read Kathleen Burns Kingsbury's latest book, *Breaking Money Silence*. Engaging, entertaining, and inspirational, *Breaking Money Silence* is a must-read for women who are ready to shatter the taboos that have held us back."

—Barbara Stanny, Author, *Prince Charming Isn't Coming:
How Women Get Smart about Money*

Breaking Money Silence®

How to Shatter Money Taboos, Talk More Openly about Finances, and Live a Richer Life

Kathleen Burns Kingsbury

 PRAEGER™

An Imprint of ABC-CLIO, LLC
Santa Barbara, California • Denver, Colorado

Library of Congress Cataloging-in-Publication Data

Names: Kingsbury, Kathleen Burns, 1966– author.
Title: Breaking money silence : how to shatter money taboos, talk more openly about finances, and live a richer life / Kathleen Burns Kingsbury.
Description: 1 Edition. | Santa Barbara : Praeger, [2017] | Includes bibliographical references and index. | Description based on print version record and CIP data provided by publisher; resource not viewed.
Identifiers: LCCN 2017024920 (print) | LCCN 2017035668 (ebook) | ISBN 9781440856594 (ebook) | ISBN 9781440856587 (alk. paper)
Subjects: LCSH: Finance, Personal.
Classification: LCC HG179 (ebook) | LCC HG179 .K55617 2017 (print) | DDC 332.024—dc23
LC record available at https://lccn.loc.gov/2017024920

ISBN: 978-1-4408-5658-7
EISBN: 978-1-4408-5659-4

21 20 19 18 17   1 2 3 4 5

This book is also available as an eBook.

Praeger
An Imprint of ABC-CLIO, LLC

ABC-CLIO, LLC
130 Cremona Drive, P.O. Box 1911
Santa Barbara, California 93116–1911
www.abc-clio.com

This book is printed on acid-free paper ∞

Manufactured in the United States of America

This book is dedicated to all the courageous people in my personal and professional life who dared to break money silence with me over the years. I am honored to have had these meaningful conversations with you and look forward to engaging in many more in the future.

Contents

Acknowledgments

Writing a book is both a solitary endeavor and a team effort. Thanks to my wonderful support system, I was able to write what was in my heart knowing that others would be there to help me each step of the way. I would like to especially thank the following friends and colleagues.

To Ken Lizotte, my literary agent, who fought diligently to find the best publisher for this book. Thank you for believing in my work and knowing there was an audience for it even when others had doubts.

To Hilary Claggett and the entire staff at Praeger, for understanding that the price people pay for money silence in our country is too high, and for trusting that I was the writer to empower readers to speak up and start talking about money matters so their lives could be richer.

To Daena Giardella, my coach, for always pushing me to be the best I can be. Thank you for believing in me as a writer, speaker, and most importantly, as a person whose voice is worth hearing.

To Lauran Star, my friend, colleague, and fellow writer, for all the pep talks and laughs over the years. Thank you for always having faith in my work and always reminding me that life is too short not to take a ski run or two at lunch.

To the KBK Team, especially Kyle Sheldon-Chandler, Mary Hanley, Marcia Greenley, and Kelly Pelissier. You are a wonderful group of powerful women who make my life easier and my work better. I share this success with you.

To Kate Victory Hannisian, for reading the book during various stages of the writing process and offering insight and suggestions that ultimately made it a better read.

To Cristen Applegate and Kaitlin Rice, my research assistants, for taking care of many of the details, so I could focus on the big picture.

And most of all to my husband, Brian, for your love and support. Being married to a writer is not an easy job and you do it with style, humor, and grace. Thank you for knowing that speaking up is my superpower.

Introduction: Being Quiet Was Never My Strong Suit

From the time I could talk, I had something to say. As a young girl, I discovered that this trait was viewed as unattractive and unladylike. Words such as opinionated, loud, and stubborn were tossed around at my expense. My elementary school report card came home with a note stating, "She talks too much to her neighbors." Even my father, who was my hero, wanted me to be quieter, and occasionally called me "the mouth." If I had listened to all these influential adults, this book would never have been written.

You see, I think speaking up, especially if you are a woman, is a good thing. How else will people know what is on your mind? You need to use tact and consider how your words may resonate with your listener. But the act of voicing your opinion and asking questions is vital to your well-being, your relationships, and your future—especially when it comes to money. Finance is the one area of life that many adults find difficult to discuss. Society tells us it's rude to ask how much someone is paid, even if he is your father or brother. You never inquire about the price of the neighbor's house, as this would be in poor taste. And even if you want to know what your friend paid for her new sports car, you bite your tongue so as to not offend. Even intimate partners, who share everything, hide purchases from each other for fear their loved one might disapprove of how they spent their money.

For someone who was born highly verbal, I too struggled to openly discuss money for many years. I found that I could proudly share when I had saved money, but not when I had made it. Like many middle-class families, mine valued thriftiness. From an early age, I was taught to save, budget, and balance a checkbook. I am grateful for these lessons, as I know many adults who didn't learn these basic skills. The money silence in my home crept in when it came to earning money and attaining success. It was okay to make a living, pay your bills, and save for retirement. But being profit-motivated was seen as distasteful.

My first job out of college was with the government and this was perfect, as I made a good living, but "not too much." I later went on to become an entrepreneur and that is when the money messages and silence in my family became a roadblock. How can you be a successful businesswoman if you are not profit-motivated? How can you know if your partner is comfortable with your financial accomplishments if you don't regularly talk to that person about money?

I learned that to grow professionally and personally, I had to open up and start talking about money. Not just about dollars and cents, but about my thoughts, feelings, and values about financial matters. The only way for me to reach the next level was to bust through my family's money taboos and start honestly talking about wealth.

I discovered that not everyone was raised to maintain money silence and that there are always exceptions to any rule. My friend Beth is one of them. She grew up in a family where finances were discussed openly. In her home, it was okay to ask how much someone earned, how much they paid for purchases, and if they were doing okay financially.

When I launched my consulting firm, Beth asked me what I was making weekly. Feeling insulted, I told her to mind her own business. Beth laughed and said she just wanted to know if I was okay and if I needed help. Perplexed but curious, I asked her to tell me more. What followed was a wonderful wealth conversation where each of us shared our viewpoints, appreciated our differences, and learned more about each other.

You see, Beth and I are friends because she doesn't like to be quiet either. The gift she gave me that night was priceless. It is a gift that I have been sharing with audiences since 2009, when I started writing and keynoting in the financial services industry on the topics of women and wealth and couples and money. Families, couples, and adults can engage in healthy money conversations. The taboo can be lifted. And when you stop being afraid, you learn so much about each other.

Breaking Money Silence is a book about how to stop keeping your thoughts and feelings about money to yourself. It is a guide for individuals, couples, and families on how to speak up, communicate, and participate in productive financial dialogues. This book is for romantic partners, whether married or living together; for parents who want to raise financially fit children; and for adult children who want to talk about finances with their aging parents. It is also a book for financial services profession-als, including bankers, CPAs, financial advisors, financial planners, estate attorneys, and wealth managers (I refer to all of these as "advisors" throughout the book), on how to embrace the human side of finance and empower their clients to engage in meaningful money conversations.

The book is divided into two sections. The first, "The Price of Money Silence," describes the financial and emotional problems caused by the long-lasting taboo against talking about money openly and honestly. It examines the very real price that women, couples, and the next genera-tion pay for keeping quiet about money matters. It also looks at the role advisors play in perpetuating money silence and how not engaging in wealth conversations with clients negatively impacts business growth and their clients' financial futures. The second section, "A Roadmap for Break-ing Money Silence," teaches you the necessary skills for having more open and effective financial conversation with your romantic partner, parents, siblings, children, and peers.

To help you put what you learn into practice, the end of each chapter has a "Money Talk Challenge." One challenge is for you and one challenge is for advisors. These challenges are coaching exercises designed to increase self-awareness around money and emotions, and provide oppor-tunities to practice new skills. I strongly encourage advisors who are read-ing this book to complete both the individual and advisor Money Talk Challenges. If this applies to you, know that gaining additional insight into your money psychology and personality will make you a more effec-tive communicator. These advisor coaching activities provide a simple way for you to incorporate breaking money silence tactics and strategies into your practice. If you are not in the financial field, but work with a professional advisor, it may be a good idea to share this book with him or her. This will create an opportunity for you to discuss the material, and the Money Talk Challenges for advisors. Also, it will help you and your advisor explore how you can communicate more openly and honestly in your work together.

As with any new skill, breaking money silence will take time to master. Be kind and gentle to yourself during this process. To increase the likeli-hood of success, carefully select whom you share these activities with. Ask individuals you trust, and if you are an advisor, work on this with clients who are most likely to be open to coaching. In time, you can prog-ress to conversations with loved ones, and/or with clients with more com-plicated interpersonal dynamics.

Money is an emotional topic that can stir up unexpected thoughts and feelings. Therefore, working with a coach or counselor trained in financial psychology as you begin breaking money silence in your life and practice can be advantageous. This allows you to learn the material, and then integrate it into your life and your business. At certain times in my journey, I have worked with coaches and counselors, and my life is richer as a result. A list of referral sources is included in the Resource Guide at the end of this book, should you decide to enlist this type of support.

I want to personally thank you for buying this book and being part of the *Breaking Money Silence* revolution. I know together, one person at a time, one couple at a time, one advisor at a time; we can change how we talk about money and end this silence for good.

Here's to speaking up!

—Kathleen

Section I: The Price of Money Silence

CHAPTER ONE

The Last Taboo: Money Talk

Money is the oil that greases the wheels of society but oil is filthy sticky stuff and we should clean our hands of it before coming out in polite society.

—Debrett's Etiquette and Style Guide, 2001

Almost half of Americans say that the most difficult topic to discuss with others is personal finance and that they would rather discuss death, politics, or religion.[1] Take a minute to let that information sink in. Many people would rather discuss dying than finances!

Turn on the television and within minutes you can find a reality show where the stars are discussing sex or drugs, two formerly taboo topics. Go to Facebook, Twitter, or YouTube and you can learn more than you care to about the food intake, relationship status, and political views of your "friends" and "followers." But ask someone you love about money and wait for the silence to set in.

Even couples who are intimate life partners have trouble talking about finances. One of my girlfriends joked, "Husbands should never know what you spend." She laughed, but the underlying message was clear: It is best not to share financial information, as you may just end up in a fight. It is hard to believe but many couples don't even know how much their significant others make for a living. A survey done by Fidelity Investments found that four out of ten people could not correctly identify their partner's salary, and 10 percent of those who did guess were off by $25,000 or more.[2] Twenty-five thousand dollars is often over half of what the average American earns. We are supposed to get married, have sex, and give birth to children, but not discuss financial matters with our partners.

Richard Tractman, PhD, a pioneer in the field of money psychology, notes, "It is the rare couple that marries these days without having at least some sexual knowledge of each other. It is quite common, on the other hand, for couples to marry without knowing anything about each other's assets or debts or discussing assumptions about who will earn the money, how it will be spent, for what, or how these decisions will be made."[3] As crazy as it sounds, this is the pact we have made and it's a bad one.

This vow of silence negatively impacts our relationships, our children, and our families. It gets in the way of proactively planning for a secure financial future. It fuels conflict and misunderstandings. It keeps women underpaid, and families from successfully passing on wealth. It contributes to the financial literacy crisis in this country, and the fact that many of our elderly live at or below the poverty level. Yet, we remain quiet.

Money is a complicated thing. In its purest form, it is a tool for commerce. It was created as a way to easily exchange goods and services. However, money means so much more. It is a symbol of love, respect, self-worth, freedom, and power. It can be used to control, reward, penalize, or entice. Having wealth is thought to bring a person great happiness. Conversely, living without it often brings great misery. Pursuing wealth can be admirable or shameful depending on whom you ask. Some believe that forgoing financial reward is noble, while others see it as foolish. For something that was designed to simplify trade, money means many things and is emotionally complex.

What does the word "money" conjure up for you? Responses vary from "comfort" and "security" to "stress" and "necessity" (see Figure 1.1). There is no right answer. But ask a few people and you are bound to get a multitude of responses. Some view money positively, like the person who stated that it conjured up "buying power." Others see it negatively, or as "a dreary necessity." This tool for commerce has become so much more. It is used as a measure of our self-worth and power, while at the same time hiding our fear and vulnerability.

I think part of the reason money talk is taboo is that internally many of us feel so conflicted about what money means in our lives, so it becomes difficult to put it into words. It is hard enough to share our emotions with others, let alone explain our feelings when they are all jumbled up. This is why understanding your own relationship with money is a vital part of breaking the money silence in your life. In Chapter 4, you will learn about your money mindset and how your money history influences its formation. A money mindset is defined as a set of beliefs about money and its purpose in your life. This mindset influences your financial habits and

Figure 1.1: What does the word "money" conjure up for you?

Exchange College Resource Tool Comfort
Necessary Freedom Necessity Security
Pay Stress Travel Needs Survival Stability
Independence

Source: Breaking Money Silence Survey for Clients, KBK Wealth Connection, 2016

your ability to talk about money with others. Until you put the pieces of your own money history together, it is almost impossible to explain your financial decisions and beliefs to someone else.

Another contributor to our collective silence about money is the barrage of mixed messages sent by our consumer-driven culture. One minute you are told that buying material goods increases your happiness, sexiness, or social status. The next minute you are scolded for carrying too much credit card debt or not saving enough for retirement. I don't know about you, but to me these messages are as clear as mud, and change with the wind.

Where did this money silence originate? Well, it is at least partly a long-standing American cultural tradition inherited from our British founders. The British aristocracy found it tasteless to discuss finances, and while America's founding fathers decided to protect their freedom of speech, they forgot to include the freedom to openly talk about money in the U.S. Constitution. Hence, the legacy of money silence followed them, and all of us, to the new land.

Some believe that wealthy families started this custom as a way to protect their fortunes. If it's rude to discuss money, then aristocrats don't have to disclose their true net worth or how they use their wealth. This custom keeps other families of lesser means in the dark, and thus the family's wealth out of harm's way. If you don't know how much the Jones family really has, then it becomes harder to steal from them.

A 2014 survey by Wells Fargo revealed the taboo against talking about money is alive and well. In this national online survey, over one thousand adults between the ages of 25 and 75 were asked to identify subjects they found most uncomfortable to discuss. Forty-four percent of Americans

surveyed found that talking about personal finance was the most challenging topic. Other uncomfortable subjects included conversations about
death (38%), politics (35%), and religion (32%).[4] It seems that almost half
of Americans would rather talk about their mortality than their financial
habits! The silver lining of these findings is that discussing politics and
religion used to be off limits, but these subjects seem to be less taboo than
in the past. Maybe there is hope for more open and honest money talk
after all.

The United States is a melting pot of cultures from around the globe, so
it is unfair to just point a finger at the British tradition. The reluctance to
talk about money seems to be a multicultural phenomenon. As people
immigrate to this country, they bring their own money taboos with them.
When a group of educated 20-somethings representing 18 countries was
asked if it is okay to inquire about someone's salary, the resounding
answer was no.

> From the Belgians to the Japanese, everyone could concur it's generally
> considered rude to ask how much money someone makes . . . The Dutch,
> Belgians and French confirmed it went against etiquette and was generally
> "not-done." The Brazilians said money is regarded as a strictly private
> affair. While admitting it's considered rather rude, the Israelis said the
> subject often comes up in conversation in their culture. The Thais all
> agreed it was taboo to bring it up.[5]

What about other types of financial conversation? Are they taboo too?
If you look at how families struggle to successfully pass down their wealth
from one generation to the next, the answer would be yes. You see, there
is a proverb in wealth management that states, "Shirtsleeves to shirtsleeves in three generations." What this means is that the first generation
creates wealth, the second generation enjoys wealth, and the third generation loses wealth. Interestingly enough, this proverb is found in almost
every culture. In Japan, it is translated as "from rice paddy to rice paddy."
In Italy, it is "from stall to stall," and in England, "from clogs to clogs."[6] It
seems that the lack of family communication about money is a global
issue and that living in a culture of money silence is a fairly universal
experience.

My Money Story

Like many people, I was inducted into the culture of money silence at
a very young age. My first money memory is from when I was five years

old. I was playing with my toy cash register and giggling each time I heard the ka-ching sound it made. I enjoyed slipping a shiny penny in the drawer and I loved money!

Only two years later, I discovered my love of money was not a good thing. My mother had sent me to the corner store to buy milk. When I returned with the milk, I neglected to give her the 10 cents in change. It was shiny and I wanted to keep it. My mother was angry and demanded the dime back, scolding me for keeping the change. Later on that year, I noticed my father's look of disappointment when I held on a little too tightly to the five-dollar bill he had given me to drop in the collection basket at church on Sunday. A sensitive kid, I quickly discovered that having and expressing my fondness for money was wrong. Money shame started to creep into my life.

At 10 years of age, I tried to bribe my mom. Knowing the power of money, I thought a quarter and a nice note might get her to say yes to my request to have a girlfriend spend the night. "Honey, you don't have to pay to get your way," my mom responded. Didn't I? Television advertisements told me that I did. To get the car, the girlfriend, or respect, it was going to cost you.

As an adult, my relationship with money was marked by ambivalence. I loved saving it and hated spending it. Of course, I married a man who was the polar opposite. For a long time our money personalities coexisted and financial disagreements were rare. We blissfully lived in money silence.

Everything changed when an unscrupulous contractor took our hard-earned money and disappeared $35,000 later, leaving us with a partially framed home addition. My money anxiety skyrocketed and my husband Brian's money avoidance deepened. I became obsessed with our finances, worrying every day about paying bills. I kept asking myself, "How could someone who is a finance major let this happen?" My husband channeled his emotions differently, which at the time I viewed as the wrong way to react. He was very angry with the contractor, and himself, but he didn't outwardly appear to be worried about money. His coping strategy was avoidance and it really ticked me off. Not knowing how to engage in a healthy financial conflict, I shut up until I blew up.

One evening I walked into the house after retrieving the bills from the mailbox. Brian was sitting on the living room couch playing video games on his Xbox. In that moment, the realization hit me. While I was fretting over the finances, he was not. I wanted to scream at the top of my lungs, but instead took a deep breath and asked, "When do you think you will start worrying about money?"

Brian looked up, put the gaming console down, and thought for a minute. He said, "When they start taking our stuff. That is when I will start worrying."

"What stuff?" I replied.

"Our television or car. You know, when they repossess our stuff."

I laughed for the first time in a while. Brian laughed with me when he realized how absurd his comments sounded.

What followed was our first honest discussion about money. We realized that while we shared money values, we had very different family money messages. I grew up in a middle-class family where the focus was on saving money and being thrifty. From my perspective, you had to have 25 percent of your annual gross income in an emergency fund or you were financially irresponsible. Brian was raised in a lower-income single parent home. They lived paycheck to paycheck. From his vantage point, if you had food on the table and a roof over your head, life was good. This conversation was the beginning of the end of the money silence in my marriage.

A Hard Habit to Break

Money is such a taboo topic that it often takes a crisis for couples or families to discuss it openly. This was the case in my family. My hope is that you (or your clients, if you are a financial advisor) don't need to reach a boiling point to talk about finances and the meaning of money and wealth in your life. It is easier to engage in this type of conversation when everyone feels less emotional. However, not talking about money is a hard habit to break.

Financial dialogues can be difficult to initiate, even for someone like me who loves to talk about taboo topics. The reasons vary from person to person and are based on family money messages and money talk mindsets. At the end of this chapter, you will complete an activity aimed at tapping into your money talk mindset. For now, know that this mindset is made up of all the thoughts, beliefs, and attitudes you have about initiating and engaging in financial conversations.

Let's look at why money talk is challenging and what makes busting through this taboo so daunting.

Money Silence Is the Social Norm

Society, families, and workplaces all reinforce the idea that money talk should be forbidden. It has been the social norm for so long that most people don't even realize that they are not engaging in these conversations. I see it all around me.

The girlfriend who won't negotiate a better price on a vacation package for fear the travel agent won't like her.

The person who gets in a skiing accident and is too afraid to ask his employer about disability benefits and goes without as a result.

The son who wants to find out if his elderly parents have enough money to live on but is reluctant to broach the subject and upset them. He thinks about their situation often but never asks them any questions.

The list goes on and on.

Our society, family money messages, and workplaces all reinforce the concept that money conversations are taboo. To speak up is to go against the norm, to potentially be seen as a problem. To be judged, often unfairly, by your peers, or worse yet, your family. Trust me, this is powerful inertia that can keep you quiet.

Talking about Money May Make You Uncomfortable

Lou Tranquilli is a financial advisor and says most people come to their first appointment feeling fearful that he will judge them for past financial behaviors. They feel exposed. He describes it as "a feeling of not living up to what the generation ahead of them has taught them to do."[7] The interesting thing is that most of the time these people are doing fine; however, they have made assumptions that their parents were better equipped to manage money. Because families typically don't talk about money, it is difficult to know if these assumptions are accurate. So many people pass judgment on themselves and then internalize a sense of guilt about money matters. According to Lou, "most people are inaccurate about whether they've done a good enough job. They just have to do maybe a little better job moving forward."

The belief is that by dodging financial conversations you can avoid uncomfortable feelings such as anxiety, incompetence, vulnerability, and fear. However, being quiet does not make these emotions go away, it just buries them underground. In the short run, you may feel better. But in the long run this avoidance catches up with you, often at a time in your life when emotions are running high anyway, such as when you are going through a divorce, facing a family health crisis, or grieving the loss of a loved one.

Financial Conversations May Involve Conflict

We live in a conflict-avoidant society that promotes the idea that fighting about money is bad and should be avoided at all costs. The truth is

that conflict is healthy and a great way to increase intimacy in a relationship. So, talking about money, and sometimes disagreeing about money,
is actually good for your marriage and your family! The dilemma is that
many people have not witnessed or experienced what it is like to fight fair
financially.

In the course of writing my earlier book *How to Give Financial Advice to
Couples*, I spoke with many people who held this belief. One interviewee
shared, "My parents always fought about money and put us kids in the
middle of those arguments. The result is I find it very difficult to talk
about money with my wife, or anyone for that matter." Others have been
able to bust this myth open, often with the help of a trusted advisor, and
view these conversations differently. As one husband put it, "When I'm
honest and open with my wife, and we talk about money, we are actually
getting closer as opposed to farther apart." This illustrates that taboos are
hard to break, but with the right help, can be shattered.

In Chapter 5, you will discover more myths about conflict and money
and will learn some guidelines for fighting fair financially.

Taboos Are Meant to Be Broken

Breaking a social taboo is never easy, but it is possible. A few decades
ago, you would not hear two people publicly discussing their religion, sex
life, sexual orientation, drug and alcohol use, or political views. Today it
is more commonplace to hear and participate in these conversations. Yes,
there are some people who still find these discussions unpalatable, but
many more, including the majority of the millennial generation, do not.
What transpired to allow these formerly forbidden subjects to be de-
stigmatized, and how do we replicate this process to break through money
silence once and for all?

I believe taboos are broken when enough people decide that the risks
associated with keeping silent are too high. For example, when parents
realized that not talking about sex with their children placed them at risk
for diseases and unwanted pregnancies, this formerly forbidden topic
became a conversation that responsible parents had with their teens. The
question is no longer *will* we talk to our kids about sex, it's *when*.

Often a taboo is broken when a handful of people revolt against the
idea that silence is golden. They decide to speak their minds. Feathers get
ruffled and those involved in the grassroots effort are criticized. Then the
media catches wind of the story and a few people talking about a topic
turns into a few thousand, then a few million. Add the power of social
media and the millions turn into billions.

Just look at the 2016 presidential election where Hillary Rodham Clinton ran against Donald Trump. Politics, a historically taboo conversational topic, became mainstream fodder. Facebook and Twitter lit up with users sharing their views. Friends and families talked more openly about their ideas at the dinner table. And it became clear that Americans had many issues to work out.

Breaking money silence will take the same grassroots-level efforts. It requires you to take a stand by daring to speak up and asking someone in your life about his or her relationship with money. It involves asking your financial services professionals to explore the emotional side of money as part of their services and reassuring them that helping you communicate about money is as valuable as the technical aspects of their work. It requires financial advisors to embrace the human side of finance and empower individuals, couples, and families to break money silence in their lives. Why make the effort? Because there is a financial literacy crisis in this country and money silence fuels it.

A recent global study found that only 57 percent of Americans passed a basic financial literacy test. The test posed questions on four main topics, including risk diversification, inflation, simple interest, and compound interest. According to the researchers, "a person is defined as financially literate when he or she correctly answers [questions on] at least three out of the four financial concepts described above." These scores put Americans at 14th place in the world on financial literacy, with Norway, Denmark, and Sweden tied for first with 71 percent of its citizens passing the exam.[8] These findings suggest that a large percentage of Americans do not possess the basic financial know-how to enable them to make sound borrowing, saving, and investment decisions. This is a depressing statistic that doesn't seem to be getting better with the next generation.

According to an annual survey by Money Matters on Campus, "On average, freshmen at four-year colleges could only answer about two out of six questions correctly about topics like the right amount of money to set aside in case of a financial emergency, the conditions placed on student loan borrowers and how long a late payment remains on your credit history."[9] If that is not a financial health crisis, I don't know what is.

We do see some efforts being made to address this problem, by organizations such as SALTMoney.org, the National Endowment for Financial Education, and the Jumpstart Coalition for Personal Financial Literacy. But what is missing from the equation is the widespread involvement of couples, families, and financial advisors. You and all the other readers of this book are the individuals who can make a difference in the fight against the taboo against talking about money. By examining your own relationship with money and learning the skills to effectively talk about financial matters personally and professionally, you will make an impact. Then take it one step further and use social media to spread the word and turn the actions of a few into a movement of many. Tweet about it on Twitter with the hashtag #breakingmoneysilence. Share it with your friends on Facebook, or post a picture of you engaging in a money conversation on Instagram. Together we can bust this money taboo wide open and start openly and honestly engaging in money talk.

Initially, it may be uncomfortable, but learning the skills to more effectively discuss money matters in your life is worth it. It will increase the intimacy in your relationships and the financial literacy of the next generation. You will discover things about yourself, your partner, your children, and your parents that help you understand why and how money is used in families and how you want it to be used in yours. If you are an advisor, you can teach clients these skills and provide a safe place for couples and families to practice these conversations. Together, one by one, we can start a revolution and end money silence for good.

This is the beginning of your journey. In Chapters 2 and 3, I will show you how and why the price you pay for money silence is too high, and then starting in Chapter 4, I will teach you the skills you need to start having healthy financial conversations with the ones you love.

Summary

In this chapter, you learned what makes talking about money with other people so complicated. Let's review the key points.

- Talking openly and honestly about money is highly discouraged in our society.
- This money taboo can be found in almost every culture around the world.
- Discussing financial matters is challenging for a variety of reasons (it goes against social norms, it brings up mixed feelings, and it may lead to conflict).
- The best time to begin a financial dialogue is when you are calm, not during a family crisis.
- The first step in breaking money silence in your life is to identify your money talk mindset.

Money Talk Challenge: Your Money Talk Mindset

All of us have a set of beliefs about financial conversations. I call this your *money talk mindset*. This set of money scripts influences how, when, where, what, and with whom you discuss financial matters. As with all mindsets, your money talk mindset is not right or wrong. But your belief system does contain valuable data about your strengths and potential blind spots when it comes to talking about financial matters.

To find out more about your money talk mindset, complete the statements below. Do not censor yourself, just put down the first response that comes to mind. If a particular situation doesn't apply to your life then skip that statement and go to the next one. The more honest you can be with yourself, the more value you will get out of this activity. If you have a willing partner, have him or her complete this exercise too, then discuss your responses and let the money conversation begin!

1. Talking about money is . . .
2. Talking about money with my romantic partner is . . .
3. Talking about money with a parent is . . .
4. Talking about money with my children is . . .
5. Talking about money at work is . . .
6. My mother taught me that talking about money is . . .
7. My father taught me that talking about money is . . .
8. My grandparents taught me that talking about money is . . .
9. My culture believes talking about money is . . .
10. My religion teaches that talking about money is . . .
11. My earliest memory of talking about money is . . .
12. The person I find the easiest to talk about money with is . . .
13. The person I find the hardest to talk about money with is . . .
14. My biggest fear when talking about money is . . .
15. If I had more money conversations, my life would be . . .

Now review your answers. Do not judge your responses; just notice any themes or trends. Write down what you discovered below.

1. Overall, my money talk mindset is . . .
2. One of my biggest strengths is . . .
3. One of my potential blind spots is . . .
4. Other things I noticed about my money talk mindset include . . .
5. One thing I would like to change about my money talk mindset is . . .

For Advisors

Complete the Money Talk Challenge above to identify your own money talk mindset. Now take a moment to consider how your personal money talk mindset may impact your professional interactions with prospects and clients.

1. How might your money talk mindset influence the type of financial conversations you have with potential and existing clients?
2. When you are working with a couple and they raise a financial difference, how might your money talk mindset influence the direction of the conversation?
3. When you are working with clients to break money silence in your office, how might your personal money talk mindset be used as a strength? How might it present a challenge?
4. What is one action you are willing to take over the next three months to help your clients break money silence in their lives?
5. Who will you tell you are taking this action and how will this person keep you accountable?

CHAPTER TWO

Silent but Deadly: The Cost of Staying Quiet

Speech is silver; silence is golden.

—Egyptian Proverb

"Take a lunch break," the waiter said as my parents laughed. I was six years old, sitting at Easter brunch at a restaurant in Virginia. As the family story goes, I was chatting away in my booster seat as my parents and sister ate their meals. Our male waiter, who apparently grew tired of my chatter, wanted me to be quiet. "Take a lunch break" was a way of him politely telling me to shut up. I don't remember if I did stop talking or not, but I do know this story has been retold in my family a million times. The not-so-subtle message was that I talk too much.

As fate would have it, I grew up and eventually became a keynote speaker and author on one of the most taboo topics, money. You see, I never bought into the idea that silence is golden.

Don't you think it's ironic that this ancient proverb equates the virtues of silence with a mineral that has been used as form of currency since 550 BC?[1] The message is loud and clear. If you want to talk about money, take a lunch break, and you will be rewarded with gold. No wonder most of us find it challenging to talk openly and honestly about money, since it's been discouraged for centuries.

But there is a cost to staying quiet. Just look at a few statistics that highlight the negative effects.

- Fifty percent of first marriages end in divorce, with financial conflict often cited as a leading cause.[2]

- Sixty-nine percent of parents feel more comfortable talking with their teens about sex than investing, contributing to the financial literacy crisis in this country.[3]
- Seventy percent of families fail to pass down wealth to future generations partially due to their discomfort with discussing finances with loved ones.[4]
- Seventy-two percent of adults report feeling stressed about money at least some of the time, with 26 percent reporting they feel financially stressed most or all of the time.[5]
- Eighty percent of spouses admit to hiding purchases from each other so they don't have to justify their spending habits.[6]

This taboo is ruining marriages and families, bankrupting businesses, and making it almost impossible for the next generation to be healthy around money. It especially harms women who are fighting for pay equity, but repeatedly are told that it's not ladylike to discuss financial matters. Not to mention its negative impact on aging parents who believe adult children should not be burdened with their financial woes.

Ironically, money silence also hurts the financial services industry and costs advisors business. Most professionals are not trained to talk about the emotional side of money and investing. Many advisors are technically strong but shy away from having in-depth discussions with you and your family about your feelings about wealth. This means if you want help having meaningful conversations about money, or need help resolving financial differences, you may be hard pressed to find a skilled advisor willing and able to provide this service. It also causes advisors to lose accounts by not proactively talking to you (their clients) about things that matter in your life, like your fears, hopes and dreams for the future, or how you want to pass down wealth to your children. The result of this oversight is that between 90 and 95 percent of the next generation (your children) leave their parents' advisors upon receiving their inheritance.[7] It certainly is easier to fire an advisor whom you have never met, or one who has not made an emotional connection with you.

I think the "lunch break" has gone on too long and it is time for all of us to stop paying such a high price for silence. For starters, let's look at how the taboo against talking about money negatively impacts you and your relationships, as well as women, and our aging population.

Couples and Money

The first thing I did when I got engaged to be married was go to the bank with my fiancé (now husband) Brian and open up a joint checking account. I just knew if we were going to spend our lives together then it made sense for me to manage (read "control") all the money. I had a degree in finance and flawless credit. He had bad debt and a propensity for spending. It was a no-brainer.

Years later, when I reflected on my relationship with money and our financial lives as a couple, I realized that my inability to trust anyone but myself with the finances was unhealthy. We didn't have money talks; instead I gave money lectures. At the time, I thought the decision for me to pay all the bills and manage all the money was a financially astute one. And if I am being really honest, I even thought being so financially put-together made me a tad bit superior. Of course, years later when we learned how to talk about money, I realized I was wrong. But at the time, this was my mindset.

My experience as a bride-to-be is not uncommon. A survey done by the National Foundation for Credit Counseling revealed that 68 percent of individuals engaged-to-be-married had negative attitudes about discussing money with their soon-to-be spouses. Five percent of those surveyed said they even would call the wedding off if they had to have a money talk.[8] No wonder half of first marriages end in divorce, with financial stress cited as one of the leading causes. Many of us start our marital lives together not discussing and agreeing on how we will save, spend, and invest money so we can live happily and securely ever after.

Until recently, the assumption was that the husband would make, manage, and invest the money, and the wife would abide by his decisions. A financial conversation prior to marriage still would have been beneficial, but seemed unnecessary due to the "traditional" gender roles which established guidelines for marital money management. Today, modern couples come into committed relationships with their own assets, debts, and earnings, and in some case, their own kids. Couples are more likely to be diverse in nature, and include same-sex couples, blended families, and co-habiting partners. Combining financial lives is far from simple and requires forethought and planning. To further complicate matters, partners have different money histories that influence their saving and spending behaviors, as well as their financial values. All these factors set the stage for financial conflict. Therefore, it is not surprising that 70 percent of married couples argue about money.[9] What *is* surprising is that partners fight about money more than they disagree about household chores, sex, and what to have for dinner.

For some couples, financial tension is minimal. Disagreements arise and are resolved. But for many more partners, financial strain contributes to relationship dissatisfaction, lack of trust, and resentment, making "happily ever after" a little less happy.

Anna, who was married for 25 years, explains how her and her ex-husband's different attitudes toward money ultimately put a wedge in their relationship. "It was a strong factor in our divorce. I can honestly say before we were married I don't think we ever had a serious conversation about money. Now I realize we viewed it very differently."

Her ex-husband grew up in an affluent family that lost their fortune suddenly. They rebuilt their wealth, but this experience heavily influenced their financial habits. "My in-laws ultimately ended up having millions but lived extremely frugally their whole life. They kept the same bedspread for probably 40 years, along with most of the items in their home. I don't think they ever got over that feeling of never knowing when it could go away."

Anna's family also experienced a loss when she was growing up, but not a financial one. Her father died in an automobile accident when she was only five years old. "My mother spent most of my childhood realizing that it can all change tomorrow and you should enjoy every minute. I think she thought it will work out and so she didn't worry—she had already experienced the worst and money was not the focus for her."

Consequently, Anna and her ex-husband had opposite family money messages and financial viewpoints. While her ex-husband always obsessed about money, worried about how much they had, and how much everything cost, she never worried about it. "I always felt that if the stock market went down, it would eventually go back up, whereas he would completely panic." The end result was they fought about money and eventually realized that their value systems were too diverse for them to remain married.

Elena also believes that financial conflicts caused her marital breakup. She was married for over 20 years, and eventually left her husband when she realized that his financial habits were not going to change. "He used money to control me and the kids. And if he did something nice for me, like buy me a gift, then the next week he would say we didn't have the money to buy groceries because he spent so much on my gift. I always felt like our money problems were my fault until I worked with a counselor and realized that I was in a no-win situation."

Another example of the price some couples pay for not talking about money is financial infidelity, defined as "deliberately and surreptitiously keeping a major secret about one's spending or finances from one's partner."[10] Examples include lying about your student or credit card debt, hiding purchases, or secretly taking out a second mortgage on the house to cover gambling debts. While these infidelities range widely in terms of their severity and impact on the relationship, all are symptoms of money silence.

Unfortunately, financial infidelity is on the rise, with 42 percent of adults surveyed in 2016 admitting to financially cheating on their partner, up from the 33 percent reported only two years prior.[11] What may start off a simple white lie or omission of truth ends up having real long-term consequences. Seventy-five percent of people who admitted to being financially deceptive say that it has affected their relationship, in ways ranging from a loss of trust to divorce.[12] For the small percentage of couples that viewed the financial infidelity as a wake-up call that they needed to talk more openly about money, the result was feeling closer to their partner.

Joanne used her credit card as a weapon against her husband John. She was tired of being married to someone who belittled her every time she needed money to buy household items or a dress for a party. "He likes having a stay-at-home wife and mother but then gets upset when I need money." Instead of directly discussing her frustrations with him, she would go shopping and run up John's American Express card balance. At the end of the month, John would get the credit card bill and they would fight about her secret shopping.

This pattern went on for about a year before the couple decided to seek marital counseling. In their sessions, Joanne learned that her financial infidelity was her attempt to have power in the relationship. It was her passive-aggressive way of expressing her anger at John for not appreciating the value she brought to the marriage and the family. John discovered that he micromanaged his wife's spending due to an unconscious fear of losing her if she was not financially dependent on him. Eventually, they both learned how to express their feelings about money, and their

Figure 2.1: The Benefits of Breaking Money Silence

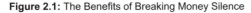

FAMILY FEUDS
FIGHTING & DIVORCE
STRESS & WORRY

FINANCIALLY FIT KIDS
BETTER RELATIONSHIPS
PEACE OF MIND

relationship improved. If they had not sought help, their money silence would have cost them their marriage.

Talking regularly with your partner about money increases intimacy and relationship satisfaction.[13] It helps you raise financially fit children and increases your financial health (see Figure 2.1). Unfortunately, the money talk taboo is so convincing in our culture, you hardly hear about the upside of financial conversations. But John and Joanne's story shows you that when partners take the risk of opening up to each other, the relationship can actually improve.

The peer pressure to remain quiet and not discuss your thoughts, beliefs, and feelings about money with loved ones is strong. However, you get to decide if the value of talking more openly and honestly about money with your loved ones outweighs the price of silence. At the end of this chapter there is a Money Talk Challenge that will help you calculate the risk and reward of breaking money silence in your life. For now, let's look at how the taboo against talking about money negatively impacts women and their financial health.

Women and Money

There has never been a time in U.S. history where women have been more economically powerful. Currently, women control over 50 percent of the personal wealth in the United States, act as primary or joint decision makers for $11.2 trillion in investable assets, and will control at least two-thirds of the nation's wealth by 2030.[14] While men still outnumber women as providers, recent studies show that 44 percent of women are the primary breadwinners in their households. Even if they don't bring home all the bacon, women make 85 percent of the buying decisions[15] and are very influential in how the family income is spent. Yes, women are a financial force to be reckoned with.

Despite this economic power, women still face financial discrimination that makes it harder for them to get paid what they are worth, access credit and business capital, and afford daily expenses. While the reasons for the gender inequities are complex, a major contributor is the mixed messages our society sends to women when it comes to money. These messages include: As a woman, you need to know about money but not be profit-motivated. You need to teach your children to be financially literate but avoid financial conflict in your life. You need to make money, but not more than your partner or spouse. It is hard enough to talk about money in our culture, but being a woman certainly adds another layer of complexity.

Lauran Star, a consultant, speaker, and author, shared a recent business experience that highlights the difference in financial expectations between men and women in the workplace. "I was asked to participate in a conference as a speaker on generational diversity, my area of expertise. I was told that they didn't have the budget to pay me but that I would receive a great deal of exposure. When I inquired as to whether the other speakers—both of them men—were getting paid, the meeting planner, who was a woman, said yes. I just couldn't resist poking the bear, so I noticed out loud the gender difference in the compensation. The meeting planner's response: 'Women were supposed to give back.' I passed on the event."

Lauran, like many women, was criticized for being profit-motivated, while men who have this trait are celebrated as go-getters. I wish Lauran's tale was the only story like this, but the truth is many women, including me, have run into this type of discrimination. The message is clear. As a woman, you are supposed to be caring and nurturing, and asking for a competitive wage just doesn't go with being feminine.

Our society's ambivalence about the role women should take in earning, managing, and investing money makes it challenging for women to assert themselves financially. This is especially true if you are from the traditional (defined as people born before 1946), or baby boomer generations (defined as people born between 1947 and 1964). You may remember a time when married women typically didn't work outside the home and could not qualify for credit without their husband's signature. (Yes, millennial generation readers, this really happened!) You may have worked your way up the corporate ladder in a male-dominated industry, only to hit your head on the glass ceiling. Or you may have become a financial advisor to make sure your female clients don't face the same monetary fate as your mother and the women before her.

Over the past 50 years, the Equal Pay Act, the Equal Credit Opportunity Act, and Title IX have been passed into U.S. law. Each one is meant to end financial inequities between the sexes. However, progress has been slow, as evidenced by the following statistics:

- Women working full-time are paid 79 cents to every dollar men working full-time are paid.[16]
- Only 4 percent of conventional small business loans go to businesses owned by women.[17]
- For people age 65 and older, more than twice as many women as men lived in poverty in 2013.[18]

It is no wonder so many women suffer in silence. The world around them has a gender bias and constantly reinforces the myth that men are better equipped to make and manage the money. Unfortunately, some financial services professionals buy into the outdated assumption that men are the financial providers and decision makers, and women aren't very interested in finances. If you have been talked down to, not invited to a financial meeting with your partner, or felt misunderstood by a financial services professional, it could be time to change to a more female-friendly advisor. The good news is there are many professionals who do understand the unique needs of women and their partners. You don't have to stay with an advisor who doesn't invest time in getting to know your unique life circumstances and financial goals.

The only way for women to change their financial reality is to speak up. Legislation and corporate change to address pay inequities are all well and good, but without individual advocacy they are not effective. I believe the tipping point will occur when both men and women break their own personal money silence and stop accepting the idea that it is okay for women to make less and pay more (for dry-cleaning services, basic clothing items, toiletries, or healthcare) simply because of their gender.

One of the major contributors to the persistent gender wage gap in the United States is that women are less likely to engage in salary negotiations than men. In fact, men are nine times more likely to ask for more money, eight times more likely to negotiate a salary offer, and four times more likely to negotiate their initial salaries.[19] The impact on women's incomes is startling. Just one year out of college, a woman working full-time earns 82 percent of what a college-educated man makes at the same point in his career. By the time a woman reaches age 60, the failure to negotiate salary can cost her up to $500,000 over a lifetime.[20] That's a steep penalty for your money silence.

The gender wage gap is only one of the issues women face when it comes to breaking their money silence. Others include the pink tax that is placed on some products and services sold to women, the cost of caring for children and elderly parents, and the gender bias in funding women-owned businesses. It seems if you were born female, you have to work a little harder to talk openly about money and live a financially secure life.

Aging and Money Silence

Did you know that 54 percent of adults admit that they would rather talk to their kids about sex than to their parents about aging?[21] The reasons for avoiding this money talk vary, but in general adult children don't want to be appear greedy or overbearing by asking mom and dad about their finances. Often siblings don't agree on when, where, and how to ask these questions. And parents don't want to admit that they may need help as their physical and mental health inevitably declines. So families remain quiet, biding their time until a crisis forces them to have this money talk.

A medical or psychiatric emergency is not the best time for families to make wise financial decisions. Emotions run high and rational thought is diminished. Even so, 85 percent of long-term care decisions are made during a medical crisis, with 70 percent of seniors needing some type of long-term care as they age.[22]

It is nice to think your family will be the exception, but the statistics are not in your favor. According to the Alzheimer's Association, the number of individuals currently suffering with this disease totals 5 million and is projected to rise to 13.8 million by 2050.[23] The average lifetime cost of care for an Alzheimer's patient is $174,000 and is estimated to grow by more than 400 percent by 2050.[24] Even if you are in the small minority of families that have good genes and dodge the Alzheimer's bullet, 50 percent of people 85 years of age and over experience some type of cognitive impairment.[25] Therefore, the likelihood that your aging parents might require some assistance with their daily finances is very high. Yet, talking to aging parents about money remains taboo.

The emotional and financial toll of not proactively talking about money as we age is great. Lack of advance planning translates into 50 percent of nursing home expenses being paid out-of-pocket and adult children contributing on average $10,000 a year to their parent's care. Add in the income lost when an adult child takes time off from work to care for mom and dad, and the price a family pays for this money silence can become astronomical.[26]

This money taboo paralyzes families of all economic statuses and cultural backgrounds. It silences parents and children, both of whom I believe are hungry for this conversation. I have seen friends, family members, and colleagues struggle with how to broach the subject with their aging parents. Conversely, I have witnessed seniors who really want to discuss finances and their end-of-life wishes with their children, but don't because it would shatter the facade that they will live forever.

Ironically, the conversation that so many families are struggling to start often brings comfort and relief when it's finally had. I know this personally. My mother struggled with Alzheimer's disease for almost a decade before she died of colon cancer. My elderly dad was her primary caregiver and, unlike many of his peers, discussed money matters with my sister and me throughout our lives. Soon after my mother's initial diagnosis, my family, with the help of a compassionate estate attorney, had an important financial conversation. We discussed my mother's wishes for care as the disease progressed, my father's desires if he should die first, and their hope for how we would continue their legacy after they were gone. It was an emotional meeting but a cleansing one. While it didn't make my mom's illness and seeing her decline any easier, it did alleviate my financial worries and concerns. I could grieve the loss of my mother without the added burden of wondering if and how my parents could afford treatment.

I was fortunate, but so many other adult children and their parents are not as lucky. Money silence keeps families tongue-tied until it's too late. If you are struggling with having this conversation with a parent, know that you are not alone. Many of the people I interviewed for this book shared stories about their attempts, some successful and some not, to discuss these matters with their aging parents. Because this is such an important and universal topic, I've devoted an entire chapter to it. In Chapter 9, I will discuss how you can begin this conversation and how a trusted advisor can help facilitate these important dialogues.

The Softer Side of Finance

When I first entered the field of financial services, I thought advisors would be excited to engage individuals, couples, and families in wealth conversations. I quickly discovered I was wrong. Most financial services professionals want to discuss your assets, incomes, and net worth. Few want to talk about money and what it means to you and your families. (Of course, if you are reading this book and work as an advisor, you are an exception to this rule.) Advisors' reluctance to discuss the emotional side of money is caused by some of the same things that block you from these conversations. A big roadblock is they live in the same money taboo society as you do.

To make matters worse, the financial services industry labels family communication the "softer" side of finance and views these services as nice to have but not necessary. Industry conferences, trade publications, and consumer magazines are chock-full of content about the technical side of money. But technical skills are only useful when combined with a keen understanding of human behavior. Topics such as raising financially savvy children, mediating financial conflicts, and helping individuals (especially women) negotiate more confidently are viewed as fluff or the icing on the cake.

Ironically, these soft skills are what separate the men from the boys when it comes to attracting and retaining advisory clients. Research shows that individuals want to work with advisors who possess high emotional intelligence and can help them communicate with their loved ones.[27] Despite this information, the industry remains focused on teaching advisors how to maximize returns and create fancy charts and graphs, over helping couples and families communicate about the human and, sometimes, emotional side of finance.

Jim Silbernagel, CFP®, is a financial planner and the creator and host of *Real Wealth*, an online radio program for insurance and financial professionals. He educates advisors and the individuals and couples he works with about the importance of family communication and strongly encourages them to participate in family meetings. His motivations are both personal and professional. "It is heartbreaking when you work with a family and once the mother and father die, the siblings never talk to each other again." He also knows that if he meets the adult children prior to their parents dying, they are much more likely to hire him as an advisor.[28]

Jim believes that it is an advisor's duty to facilitate these dialogues before it's too late and is frustrated with those in his field who don't make it a priority. "My industry is as guilty as the families when it comes to money silence. Advisors don't want to rock the boat, they just want to make sure they get business done."[29]

If financial services professionals are not being trained and encouraged to break money silence in their offices, what about mental health and marriage and family counselors? As a former psychotherapist, I can assure you that the money taboo runs just as wide and deep in the helping professions.

For 15 years, I worked as a licensed mental health counselor in private practice. It was challenging but deeply rewarding work. It is also a world where money silence runs rampant. Highly respected and skilled therapists would take the most difficult cases and barely be compensated for their work. During my tenure, insurance companies simultaneously increased the required paperwork and reduced compensation rates for therapists. My colleagues would periodically complain about these pay cuts and the injustice of it. But collectively they would remain quiet about how this reduction in pay negatively impacted their own financial well-being. At times, the silence about money was so loud I could hear it.

In 1999, Richard Trachtman, PhD, wrote a groundbreaking article titled, "The Money Taboo: Its Effects in Everyday Life and in the Practice of Psychotherapy." In it he stated that money "is perhaps the most ignored subject in the practice, literature, and training of psychotherapy."[30] More recent studies have found that "compared to other occupations, mental health professionals report significantly lower levels of financial health," and are more likely to be money avoidant.[31] This translates into a field full of helping professionals uncomfortable with, and in some instances not skilled in, money matters. Not surprisingly, money conversations are often sidestepped in therapy sessions.

Every field has its own money mindset. A money mindset is how you think and feel about money and its purpose in your life. The counseling profession believes whole-heartedly in the nobility of poverty. To be profit-motivated is evil. To be selfless is revered. The outcome of these money attitudes is that many practitioners avoid discussing their fees, fail to collect past due payments from insurance companies, and live in financial chaos. Therefore, talking with their patients about how money attitudes and experiences impact their mental health is a charged topic for professionals who have yet to explore their own mixed emotions around finances.

Conversely, the financial services industry has a money mindset that clearly says asset size matters. Services are only provided to individuals and families with wealth, and those with modest resources are considered a waste of the advisor's time. Poverty is shameful; affluence is admirable. This money attitude, while the polar opposite of the counseling profession's, also fuels money silence. While it is okay to talk about how to accumulate wealth, discussions around the emotional side of money and its meaning in one's life are discouraged. This discouragement is not always overt, but implied, as these topics rarely make an advisory meeting agenda.

From my perspective, the counseling and financial fields have more in common than they think. They both are victims of money silence. Professionals from both industries fail to provide individuals, couples, and families with a safe place to discuss their emotions about money and wealth. To do so, advisors and therapists need to start by exploring their own relationship with money. However, this is a dilemma, as counselors equate focusing on money with being greedy and advisors equate focusing on feeling with being soft.

The answer lies in both these professions joining together and learning from each other. Fortunately, for all of us, some organizations are trying to do just that. The Financial Therapy Association is dedicated to bringing researchers, financial professionals, and counselors together so they can learn from each other. The Purposeful Planning Institute, founded by a self-proclaimed "recovering lawyer," is also focused on gathering professionals from different disciplines to help families and professionals engage in healthier dialogues. Both organizations are breaking new ground, but the progress they are making is slow.

My hope is that reading this book will help you explore your relationship with money and bust through the money silence in your life. Whether you are a consumer, counselor, or advisor, your role in shifting how society thinks and feels about money conversations is vital.

Join the Revolution

Changing human behavior takes time and one or two organizations can't do it all. To really shatter the money taboo in our society, each and every one of us needs to make a commitment to doing more. It starts with exploring your own relationship with money and assessing the cost of money silence for you and your family. Then you can learn new communication skills so you can talk more openly and honestly about money in your own life. For advisors, this has a trickle-down effect. By walking the walk, you are serving as a role model to individuals and couples that busting money taboos is possible. Furthermore, having been through the process, you can show them how it is done.

For me, not talking about money led to years of underearning and guilt about spending money. I realized the emotional and financial price was too high. At first it was not easy to get the dialogue started. But now that I have spoken honestly with my husband, family, and friends, I have richer relationships.

Over the last decade, I have spoken to thousands of professionals on the topic. Whether I am presenting to an audience full of bankers, business owners, counselors, financial advisors, lawyers, or women, the discussion and questions are similar. People ask me "How do I begin a money conversation?" "What can I expect to feel?" and "What happens if the other person won't engage in the dialogue?" The answers may be different for each of us, but the process of speaking up is the same. All you need to get started is a healthy dose of curiosity and a firm conviction that the price you have been paying to stay silent is too high.

Summary

In this chapter, you learned the high price you and your loved ones pay for money silence. Here are some things to remember.

- Money silence contributes to the high divorce rate and the low financial literacy scores in the United States.
- Parents struggle to successfully pass down wealth to the next generation partially due to the lack of good financial communication skills in families.

- Money silence negatively impacts an adult child's ability to care for an aging parent.
- Woman are especially harmed by money silence as they fight for pay equality.
- Partners (and loved ones) who regularly engage in money talk report more intimate and satisfying relationships.

Money Talk Challenge: The Price You Pay for Money Silence

Answer the following questions to gain insight into which money conversations are more difficult to hold with your loved ones, and the price you pay for staying silent. If it helps, select one person in your life to think of as you answer these questions. This could be a parent, partner, child, or sibling. For example, if you decide to use a parent, then the first question would be, "What is one financial topic you find easy to discuss with your parent?"

1. What is one financial topic that you find easy to discuss?
2. What makes talking about this money matter comfortable?
3. What can you learn about this money conversation that you can use when discussing more difficult topics?
4. What is the one financial topic that is most uncomfortable to discuss?
5. What makes talking about this money matter uncomfortable?
6. On a scale of 1 (lowest) to 5 (highest), rate your comfort level when discussing this difficult money matter.
7. What would have to happen for this rating to increase by ½ point? 1 point?
8. If you never talk about this matter, what is the potential financial cost to you? To your partner? To your family?
9. If you never talk about this matter, what is the potential emotional cost to you? To your partner? To your family?
10. What action will you take in the next week to reduce the price you pay for money silence in your life?

For Advisors

Answer the questions above from the perspective of being a professional working with clients. Review your answers and then complete the following statements.

1. My money silence about_____(insert your most difficult topic) may cost my clients by . . .

    Example: Planning for Chronic Illness. My money silence may cost my clients an opportunity to reduce their expenses relative to healthcare and it may cost them some emotional stress if they have to figure this out while a loved one is seriously ill.

2. My money silence about _____ (insert your most difficult topic) may cost my business by . . .

    Example: Not helping clients discuss chronic illness could cost me future referrals and be a roadblock to retaining the healthy spouse.

3. The one small action I am willing to take today to break money silence with my clients is . . .

    Example: I will discuss this with my business coach in our next meeting.

CHAPTER THREE

All Men Are Financially Literate and Other Myths about Gender and Money

Money speaks but it speaks with a male voice.
—Andrea Dworkin, American feminist and author

Over the past decade, I have been invited to speak to audiences of financial advisors, bankers, and wealth managers in the United States and internationally on the topics of women and wealth and couples and money. The reason I am so busy is that the financial services industry has a big problem when it comes to attracting and retaining women and their partners as clients. My company, KBK Wealth Connection, offers consulting, training, and tools for helping firms and advisors become more gender-savvy and communicate about financial matters more effectively.

I love what I do, but at times it can feel like an uphill battle. Many firms talk the talk but fail to take real, meaningful action that will result in a more gender-savvy organization. Sometimes I feel like I am working back in an idealized version of the 1950s, where all men provide for the family and all women stay at home to care for the kids. You and I both know this is not the case at all today (nor was it entirely the case back in "the good old days"), but some of the people who help you manage your money sometimes forget because they work in a male-dominated industry which simply needs to catch up with the times.

One of the most glaring examples of this outdated mindset surfaced in early 2015 when I was hired to speak on the main stage at a bankers' wealth and trust management conference. Minutes before I stepped on stage, I discovered that I was the first female keynoter in their 140-year history! I was honored and horrified. Yes, I was breaking barriers at this organization, but the lack of women keynoters was a red flag pointing to the industry's fundamental problem. How can you attract and retain affluent women and their partners as clients, and talented women as employees, if you don't show them that they matter by having someone who looks like them on stage at the conference?

More recently, I was invited to keynote at a retirement symposium. Part of my standard preparation for any engagement is to ask the meeting planners and potential audience members for questions they would like answered in my talk. When I received the list of questions it read like a script from the 1950s television sitcom *Leave It to Beaver.* All the questions inferred that women were financially dependent on their wealth-creating husbands and disengaged from family financial matters. Conversely, the meeting planners seemed to believe that the husbands were financially literate, passionate about investing, and involved. What struck me was how this talented, well-meaning group of advisors was unaware of how their assumptions reinforced traditional gender stereotypes about men, women, and couples. Unfortunately, this experience is more common than you might think.

Financial services professionals are not the only ones who fall into gender traps. Most of us do. Beliefs such as "all men are financially literate" and "all women are not interested in investments" are commonplace in our society. These overgeneralizations based on outdated stereotypes make men *and* women feel as if they are very different from each other when it comes to money. The truth is that we are all human beings and not so diverse when it comes to difficulties talking about money. Money silence is an equal opportunity issue that affects both sexes. The problem with gender myths is they zap our curiosity and fuel misunderstandings. Yes, every stereotype has a kernel of truth, but you need to discover if and how it applies to you and the people around you, as opposed to simply assuming it does. Let's look at common gender myths and how they might impact your relationship with money and your loved ones.

Myths about Women and Wealth

Despite all the facts and figures indicating otherwise, women are generally viewed as less financially competent than men. Misconceptions about female breadwinners, women business owners, and women who stay at home to raise children abound. These myths contribute to women not seeing themselves as financially astute or downplaying their financial know-how, and their advisors not meeting their needs. These financial fallacies need to be replaced with the facts if women are going to break money silence in their lives.

Below are five common myths about women and money, and how they contribute to financial misunderstandings and money silence.

Myth 1: Women Are Not as Financially Literate as Men

The truth is that women are just as financially literate as men, as evidenced by the fact that 35 percent of women versus 39 percent of men in the United States passed a basic financial literacy assessment. Yes, only four percentage points separated the sexes, but women are still labeled as less knowledgeable. The sad fact is that almost 60 percent of adults (men and women) cannot pass a basic financial literacy exam.[1] Instead of just focusing on the need for more women to learn about money and investing, we need to understand that the real story is that our country has a financial literacy crisis that isn't getting adequate attention.

The mortgage loan crisis in 2009 serves as a good example of how many Americans made bad decisions due to their lack of financial literacy. While the media blamed the banks and mortgage companies for misleading consumers, that was only part of the overall problem. It was also the fact that many consumers (both men and women) didn't have the financial knowledge to realize that taking out a mortgage with little to no equity was a bad decision. Savvy homebuyers know that it is standard to put a 20 percent deposit toward the price of a home to protect themselves from owing the bank more than the home is worth, in the event the value of the property drops while they own it.

The lack of financial knowledge is an equal opportunity problem. But still our society, the financial services industry, and the media all focus more on women's shortcomings financially as opposed to all Americans' challenges. One reason is women are more willing than men to admit when they don't feel confident about their financial knowledge. Unfortunately, this underlying reason is often ignored and therefore, women are thought to be the less financially literate gender.

In our culture, women are socialized to show their weaknesses and connect with others when they are vulnerable. Conversely, men are taught to hide their vulnerabilities and practice a "fake it until you make it" approach to interacting with others. This gender difference is a key reason why as a group, women report a lower level of financial confidence. They are not necessarily less knowledgeable, just more likely to admit when they need help. But isn't asking for help a strength? Not in the male-dominated world of finance.

In the financial industry, men are depicted as financially literate and self-assured investors. Women are described as financially challenged and timid investors. This view then turns into a self-fulfilling prophecy. Think about it. If you are repeatedly told that you are not good with money, you may just not even try to manage your personal finances. And if you are looking for a career, you are less likely to pursue this area of study. Why would you? Your strengths are ignored and your weaknesses exploited. The myth that women are not as financially literate as men makes it less likely that women will work with financial advisors, or pursue careers in financial planning or a related profession. This is one reason that only 23 percent of Certified Financial Planners are women.[2]

It is time to realize that there is a financial literacy crisis in this country that affects all of us. The impact keeps both men and women from receiving the education and support they need to live financially balanced and healthy lives. Besides, it's easier to talk about money matters with your loved ones and employers when you understand the building blocks that make up a solid financial foundation.

Myth 2: Women Are Not Really Interested in Finance

I hear this myth all the time when I speak at industry conferences. The questions posed vary, but the underlying sentiment is that women are not really interested in finance and it's the advisor's job to get them to care about money matters. But the facts don't support the idea that women are disinterested. In fact, 92 percent of women want to learn more about financial planning and 83 percent want to get more involved in their finances within the next year.[3] Therefore, the idea that women as a group are not interested in their financial lives is simply not true.

When Mark and Wendy met with a new advisor, he only spoke with Mark. After the appointment, Wendy called me up to complain about the meeting. "Can you believe that the advisor assumed that because I am a woman I don't know anything about money and investments?" she asked. I assured her that unfortunately her experience was not unique. "But I manage a mutual fund. He didn't even bother to ask me what I did for a living." It was true. She was in the industry and knew much more about investments than her husband Mark did.

If only the advisor had asked one "curious question," he might have landed this new business. Instead he assumed that Wendy was not really interested in finance and that Mark made the investment decisions.

Why does this myth live on? I think it's because it's convenient for many in the financial services industry to hold onto this falsehood. It allows professionals to see the client as the problem, as opposed to facing a harsh reality about themselves. Fifty percent of the population, women, don't like the traditional, transactional approach historically employed by financial service institutions and professionals. Instead of looking at how advice and services can be tailored to better meet the needs of different client segments and train all financial services professionals to be more gender-savvy, the industry blames women.

I realize if you are a professional reading this book, this statement probably doesn't apply to you. But my guess is it may resonate with what you see as a member of the industry. The good news is slowly, more banks, financial firms, and wealth management companies are embracing a more female-friendly, gender-savvy approach to client service. In time, this myth will be debunked for good.

Myth 3: Women Are Overly Emotional Investors

As an expert in financial psychology, I find this is one of my favorite myths. It speaks to the emotional side of money and the area I think financial advisors need to work on the most. While women are more likely to express their feelings about investments, retirement, and their financial future, all human beings get emotional about money from time to time. Just because men tend to keep their feelings to themselves does not mean they aren't experiencing stress, worry, or anxiety too. And just because women verbalize these feelings doesn't necessarily mean that women are being overly emotional.

Bridget, a 55-year-old mother of two adult children, is a great example of how women can get labeled as too emotional when it comes to money. Bridget worries about having enough money to retire and fears that she may become a burden to her children as she ages. When she brings this topic up with her partner, he insists she is overreacting. When Bridget shares her concerns with their advisor during a joint meeting, the advisor shows her an Excel spreadsheet with numbers and projections and assures Bridget that she and her husband will be fine. "Don't worry so much. That is why you have me," the advisor replies. Bridget's emotions are again minimized.

What both her husband and her advisor don't understand is that Bridget's feelings are normal. Emotions such as the fear of running out of money or being a financial or emotional burden to the next generation are common for women contemplating retirement. Bridget is not "overly emotional," she is just simply looking for a safe place to discuss these feelings.

The problem lies in the financial services industry. It is a highly technical field that has brainwashed all of us into believing that managing money is a purely rational endeavor. But the truth is making, managing, and investing money is both a rational and an emotional pursuit. It just so happens that women have been socialized to excel at tapping into their emotions related to money and, therefore, to identify and want to talk about these feelings. Most female investors take a little longer to make a financial or investment decision because they want to discuss their feelings, and bounce ideas off their friends and family. Instead of making them "too emotional," such behavior actually leads many women to be balanced investors who realize long-term rates of return similar to, if not better than, those achieved by their male counterparts.[4] Research shows that men tinker with their investment portfolio 50 percent more than women and are more likely to chase a hot stock tip or try to time the market.[5] Ironically, men may actually be more emotionally reactive investors than women.

Either way, it is human to have feelings related to money. It is time for the world of finance and our society to accept that finance and investing is emotional business.

Myth 4: Women Are Risk-Averse

The traditional definition of risk looks only at return relative to the potential for financial loss. However, women typically evaluate investment risk more holistically. It is not just about the numbers, but about whether they feel confident in their decision and how that decision may impact their family life. So, when women want to talk about risk and consult with others before investing, it is often mislabeled as women being afraid to take risks with their money. In reality, they are just more likely to take into account all the potential risks before making a decision.[6]

Sherri Munro, owner of Munro Consulting Services, worked in commercial lending for almost two decades and now coaches women entrepreneurs at various stages in their businesses. Sherri has noticed that some banks tend to assume that women don't want to grow or scale their businesses and that they are fearful of the risks necessary to do so. She observes how this ultimately hurts the financial institution and the women they are trying to serve. "In the past, banks regularly have done one (or all) of these three things: they categorize women entrepreneurs by what they don't do, therefore limiting the complexity of advice or options that are discussed (i.e., 'non-borrowing'); they ineffectively manage the relationship (i.e., personal or small business expertise versus commercial expertise); or they fail to make introductions or consider other professionals who could help the business grow considerably (i.e., equity financing options, venture capital)." The result is women entrepreneurs are unsatisfied and underserved consumers, and financial institutions end up missing out on a business growth opportunity.

Women-owned businesses are funded at a lower rate than those run by men. Loan approval rates for women-owned small businesses are 33 percent lower than they are for male-owned enterprises.[7] And between 2010 and 2015, only 10 percent of venture capital dollars globally went to fund startups with a female founder, meaning 90 percent of all venture capital went to men.[8] Part of the reason is the way risk is defined by the financial industry versus the way women think of it. For too long, women have been labeled as scared to invest in themselves or their businesses, when in fact they are just weighing all the factors, and calling on advisors to engage in a more in-depth conversation before saying yes to their recommendations.

Myth 5: Women Are Not Profit-Motivated

Modern women receive mixed messages about earning money and being profit-motivated. The modern woman is not supposed to be financially dependent on a man as "he could leave you for a younger woman/ someone else at any time." However, you (as a woman) are not supposed to be profit-motivated because it might make the men and other women in your life uncomfortable. Believe it or not, 40 percent of women think that being financially independent would make them intimidating and unattractive to men, and one-third believe it can alienate other women.[9]

In 2012, Marissa Mayer accepted the position of CEO at Yahoo when she was six months pregnant. The buzz in the media and by the watercooler was about how could she put her career and profit ahead of her unborn child. Articles, social media posts, and conversations about the pros and cons of women working at this level ensued. Some thought accepting this job was selfish and would make Marissa a less effective mother and a less impactful CEO. No matter where you stand on this issue, our society is clearly not comfortable with a woman being in a powerful leadership position. Would the same outrage have occurred if Marissa was named Matt and his wife was expecting a child when he took the position? I can safely say the answer to that question is no. It is acceptable for men to be career-driven and profit-motivated but not women, especially those women who want to be mothers too.

Women are socialized to be relationship-oriented and to put other people's financial needs ahead of their own. Whether it is your son's desire to go to hockey camp, your partner's interest in taking flying lessons, or your mother's request for a loan, you are expected to put their desires first. Your needs, like saving for retirement or maybe taking a long-overdue trip to the spa, are supposed to be put on the back burner. It is a dilemma, because if you do prioritize yourself or admit to enjoying making money, you are often criticized. Worse yet, you are seen by some as not desirable as a mate. It is no wonder so many women struggle to break money silence.

In reality, if you enjoy making money, are profit-motivated in your business, or want a high return on your investment portfolio, this is a sign you are financially savvy. These desires have nothing to do with your attractiveness, and if a potential mate thinks so, it may be time to find a new one. Practicing financial self-care should not threaten your ability to find a life partner and live happily ever after.

In the Money Talk Challenge at the end of this chapter, you will have a chance to identify and debunk other myths about women and wealth. For now, let's turn to the other side of the coin and discuss the falsehoods about men and finance.

Myths about Men and Money

While financial fallacies about men are discussed less often, they are as embedded in our society as myths about women and wealth. These myths put pressure on men to appear more knowledgeable than they may be, and can prevent open and honest money conversations with their loved ones and advisors.

Below are some common myths about men and money and how they contribute to the financial misunderstandings and money silence.

Myth 1: Men Are Financially Savvy

The societal expectation is for men to be the financially savvy ones in relationships. However, many men prefer to let their partners, wives, or girlfriends handle the money. The reasons vary from person to person and range from having a partner who has an interest or expertise in finance to not being interested or skilled in money management. Sound familiar? Yes, men have many of the same reasons women do for deferring their financial responsibilities.

Rose complained to me during an interview for my book *How to Give Financial Advice to Couples* that her husband Charlie refused to learn about the family finances. Rose, by default, is the person who meets with the financial advisor and makes investment decisions for the couple. "Charlie just isn't interested in money matters. No matter how many times I ask him to join me for meetings with our advisor or to help me balance the household checkbook, he refuses. It is like he is another one of my kids when it comes to finance." According to Rose, Charlie feels it is too late to become financially literate and that as long as he is married to her he will be fine. Couples like Rose and Charlie are more common than you think. In my experience, men don't always know about or enjoy finance, but they tend to talk about it less, allowing their lack of literacy to fly underneath other people's radar.

This myth makes it more difficult for men to speak up and ask questions about financial matters. Some men stay quiet because they fear being judged by society, and financial advisors, for not being more astute. It is vital for society to let go of these judgments so men can feel more comfortable talking openly about money with their partners, their children, and their advisors.

Myth 2: Men Are Confident Investors

Confident investors are knowledgeable and have the insight and emotional intelligence to make sound investment decisions. While some men are confident in this area, as are some women, there is a tendency for men to be overly confident, which has a negative impact on their portfolio's financial performance. This phenomenon was first discussed in the classic behavioral research study, "Boys Will Be Boys: Gender, Overconfidence and Common Stock Investment." The researchers, Barber and Odean, discovered that male investors were more likely to trade on a hot stock tip or attempt to time the market based on overconfidence in their abilities. The men paid more trading fees than their female counterparts and rarely outwitted the market. Their overconfidence led to lower long-term returns than those of female investors, who typically traded less frequently.[10]

Part of the masculine tendency to act as if you are knowledgeable stems from how boys are socialized to not display what society may view as weaknesses. Thus, many men ask fewer questions in advisory meetings and give the appearance in public of being more financially knowledgeable than they are. They fear showing vulnerability when it comes to money matters. This lack of transparency hurts them and their loved ones. Instead of asking for help or clarification, they hide their ignorance. For some, it costs them and their families money as they invested poorly.

Myth 3: Men Like to Control the Family Finances

When I was writing my book *How to Give Financial Advice to Couples*, I discovered how outdated this belief really was. Many of the women I interviewed for that book shared their frustrations that they could not get their husbands to take an active role in financial matters. One interviewee really wanted her partner to attend advisor meetings with her, but he refused. "He just wanted to keep his head in the sand about money," she said. This sounds a lot like a complaint many of us would think a man would make about his wife. But times are changing and gender doesn't determine your interest in overseeing the family finances.

Couples from the millennial generation have a greater propensity to manage their money together and share financial responsibilities.[11] This trend may be a result of more partners coming to their relationships with established careers and incomes. With more women becoming the primary breadwinners for families, this trend is likely to continue. This money myth puts some men in precarious positions, as there continues to be societal pressure for them to control, or at least appear to oversee, the family finances. Privately they might enjoy sharing this task, or want to relinquish it completely, but publicly they must act differently. Again, men are pushed into a "fake it until you make it" scenario, as opposed to being able to be who they are financially. This makes it challenging to have an authentic relationship with money and transparently discuss finances with others.

Myth 4: Men Are Money-Motivated

During an April 2014 meeting about gender pay inequality, Will Infantine, a State House Representative from New Hampshire, said, "Men are more motivated by money than women are."[12] This statement made national headlines as it was not backed by facts, but spoke to the general sentiments that many in our society believe. While women make an average of 79 cents to every man's dollar,[13] the reasons are complex and certainly cannot be fully explained by this imaginary difference in money motivation between the sexes.

The truth is some men are money-motivated and some are not. Men who are profit-motivated tend to select careers that reinforce this trait such as finance, business, and sales. However, many men select careers based on their interest in helping others and/or solving a problem. These guys end up in counseling, healthcare, engineering, or academia.

As a coach, I have worked with men who have avoided asking their clients or employers for money, or who prefer to let their partner be the primary financial provider. These men are driven but in different ways. My husband Brian is a great example of a man who is career-driven but not money-motivated. He has a good work ethic and takes pride in helping his customers reach their goals. But I have never seen him make a career decision based on the promise of a higher salary. When he considers a job opportunity he looks for like-minded coworkers and a position that allows him to bike after work. When we first got married I thought he was joking about taking a position at a new firm and making the final decision based on the proximity to the mountain bike trails. I now know that his love of adventure is a core value and no amount of money would convince him to give up his daily mountain bike ride.

Myth 5: Men Talk to Other Men about Investments

Recently I was presenting to a group of women business owners at an association meeting. As the group discussed the challenges they faced as female entrepreneurs, the topic of men talking about money came up. One woman complained, "Men talk about money all the time and learn from each other. They have an unfair advantage." There happened to be two brave businessmen at this women's event, so I asked them if that statement was true. Their response, "Some men do. Some men don't." One man shared his belief that men wait too long to let other men know about financial matters, especially when they are in financial trouble or have made a bad investment. In his opinion, by the time his male friends break their money silence, the losses have begun or the damage has already been done.

Money conversations can be difficult for both men and women. Those who do engage in these dialogues were either raised in a family that encouraged money talks or learned this skill from the school of hard knocks. The assumption that all men are sharing stock tips and financial information on a regular basis is not based in reality. The men in financial services and banking may do so, but most men do not. They need the same help as women do to open up about financial matters.

When you look at this list of myths about men and money, what is your reaction? Do you see yourself buying into these false beliefs from time to time? As with the stereotypes about women and money, these generalizations need to be replaced with the facts. Financial knowledge and insight is not determined by your gender. Rather, it is shaped by the amount of financial education you receive, your unique money history and family money messages, and your interest in investments and money matters. Your relationship with money is nuanced and gender is only one small part of the puzzle.

A More Gender-Savvy World

The one-dimensional lens used to financially view men and women needs to be widened. This requires all of us—whether you are an individual, member of a couple, parent, adult child, or financial professional—to examine our automatic thoughts and beliefs about gender and money. Understanding key gender differences as they relate to wealth is important, but only to inform real-life conversations. For example, the tendency of many women to view wealth holistically and want a collaborative approach to working with an advisor is useful data. But this does not mean that all women relate to wealth and their advisors in this fashion. To truly connect with someone, it's important to ask curious, open-ended questions aimed at discovering what makes the other person in the dialogue tick.

Here are a few tips to help you and those around you live in a more gender-savvy world.

Be Inclusive

Being gender-savvy includes both sexes and also those who identify as gender fluid. It means accepting and celebrating our differences and our commonalities. When it comes to talking about money, it helps to be curious about how the other person makes financial decisions and views the purpose of wealth in his or her life. Use gender as a foundation to launch from, not a place to land. Fight the urge to pigeonhole partners, parents, children, and siblings by gender, or to advise clients based solely on their sex. Instead, practice being open-minded and accepting of all the wonderful nuances each of us brings to our relationship with money and the world.

Ask Curious Questions

It is so easy to slip into assumptions about women and men, especially when you are romantically involved or have a long history together. Fight the urge to read someone's mind, and practice curiosity in its place. Bring a sense of wonder to every money talk and work diligently to put yourself in the other person's shoes. Trust me, there is a lot we could learn from people who don't share our perspective on money matters.

Seasoned financial advisors may struggle with curiosity a bit more than those newer to the field because they have witnessed many client situations that appear to resemble each other. In the next section of the book, "A Roadmap for Breaking Money Silence," we'll explore this concept in depth. For now, know that if you enter every conversation with some questions, without any preconceived answers, it will serve you well.

Know Language Matters

A few years ago, I worked with a great group of men at a wealth management conference. Our values and beliefs about what advisors needed to learn to better serve their clients and grow their businesses were aligned. But every time they referred to their female colleagues as girls, I cringed.

Words send a powerful message to the people around you. Even the word "girls" may seem benign but can be offensive to the women you work with. It implies entitlement or thinking of others as "less than"— men are men, women are girls. And while personally I find it a lot less upsetting than many women I know, using the word "girls" in that context did leave a bad impression. It's better to err on the side of caution than to guess which terms will be perceived as insensitive or offensive.

Hire for Gender Diversity

The Global Leadership Forecast in 2014/2015 surveyed 2,000 global organizations across all industries and found that the companies that had the best financial performance had twice as many women in leadership positions.[14] It just makes good business sense for companies to become gender-savvy in their hiring practices. I realize this can be harder than it sounds. What is important is this issue is being discussed and attempts are being made to improve the diversity at companies across the board.

If you are a leader or owner of a company, consider putting diversity hiring policies into place and offering diversity training for your employees. If you work at a company, talk to your peers, your human resource department, or the leadership team and advocate for more inclusive and diverse hiring practices. In financial services, the Certified Financial Planning Board formed a Women's Initiative Network to tackle this issue, so consider supporting their work by visiting their website at http://www

.cfp.net/. Click on the "About CFP Board" tab and select "CFP Board's Women's Initiative (WIN)" from the drop-down menu.[15]

Be a Role Model

The world needs more gender-savvy role models and I think *you* are perfect for the part. Role models include mothers, fathers, aunts, uncles, co-workers, bosses, community leaders, and teachers. All it takes is a commitment to learning as much as you can about gender bias and proactively discussing these matters with other people in your professional or personal life.

If you are a wife, mother, aunt, or daughter, educate those around you and let them know these gender myths are outdated. If you are a husband, father, uncle, or son, show other men that opening up about money is a wise thing to do. If you are a financial advisor, advocate for real change in the financial services industry by creating products and services that are based on the facts, not outdated fallacies. Offer opportunities for clients to discuss these myths with you and each other. If we all do our part, we can live in a more gender-savvy world.

Summary

In this chapter, you learned about gender money myths, how these stereotypes fuel money silence, and steps to take to be more gender-savvy. Let's review the key points to remember.

- Money silence is an equal opportunity issue that impacts both sexes.
- Gender myths about money contribute to financial misunderstandings between people, and advisors and clients.
- It is normal for both men and women to experience feelings about their finances from time to time.
- It is important to be open-minded and ask curious questions to learn more about another person's money mindset.
- Advocate for gender diverse hiring practices at work and role model gender-savvy behaviors at home.

Money Talk Challenge: Gender Myth Scavenger Hunt

You may not realize it, but myths about gender and money can be found everywhere in our society. They can even be found in places you would not think to look, such as the lyrics of a song, a scene in a movie, or in personal and professional conversations. This Money Talk Challenge

Table 3.1   Gender Myth Scorecard

Places to Look	Gender Myth	Gender Truth
Book		
Grocery Store		
Movie		
Music Video		
Newspaper Article		
Personal Conversation		
Radio		
Retail Store		
Self-Talk		
Song Lyrics		
Television Show		
Website		
Work Conversation		
Video Game		
Other . . .		

is geared to opening your eyes to all the gender myths around you, and realizing how noticing them can create opportunities to discuss these misconceptions with others.

Instructions

Pick one day to go on a gender myth scavenger hunt. Use the chart (see Table 3.1) as a guide to where to look for these messages. These are some of the places you might find misconceptions about gender and money mentioned or portrayed. Feel free to add more places to the chart. Over the course of the day, write down on the chart all the gender myths you hear, see, or observe. The goal of this scavenger hunt is to find as many gender myths about money as you can. While you can do this exercise on your own, it is more fun to invite friends, family, or coworkers to join you.

At the end of the 24 hours, review this list and write down one gender truth for every gender myth about money that you encountered. Then answer these questions.

1. What was the most surprising place(s) you found gender myths?
2. How might these gender myths influence how you think and feel about money?

3. How might these gender myths impact how you talk to others about money?

4. What was it like to challenge these myths?

5. What is one thing you will do differently as a result of this exercise?

If you completed this scavenger hunt with other people, set aside 30 minutes in the next week to discuss your observations and to learn from each other. Make it fun and give the person with the most myths and reframed truths a prize!

For Advisors

Complete the client Money Talk Challenge above. If you have a staff, do this as a team exercise and then discuss it at your next team meeting. Next, apply what you learned from that activity and this chapter to your work with clients. Start by observing when you are curious about clients and when you fall into the trap of making assumptions based on gender stereotypes. This self-awareness will be useful in avoiding these pitfalls going forward.

To be more gender-savvy in your approach to assessing clients' financial literacy and confidence levels, use some or all of the following questions in your discovery meetings.

1. On a scale of 1 (lowest) to 5 (highest), rate your current financial literacy. Financial literacy is defined as having the knowledge and skills to make and manage your financial resources now and in the future.

2. If you could pick your ideal literacy rating, what would it be and why?

3. What would have to change for you to reach that number?

4. How can I help you as an advisor achieve that ideal rating?

5. On a scale of 1 (lowest) to 5 (highest), rate your current level of confidence in making good financial decisions.

6. If you could pick your ideal confidence rating, what would it be and why?

7. What would make your confidence rating go up one point?

8. What, if anything, would make your confidence rating go down one point?

9. What else do you want me to know about your financial literacy and confidence?

10. How can I help you reach your ideal financial literacy and confidence ratings?

When advising couples have each partner complete this exercise separately then have them compare their answers.

Section II: A Roadmap for Breaking Money Silence

CHAPTER FOUR

It Is Not about the Price of Milk

The greatest conflicts are not between two people but between one person and himself.

—Garth Brooks, American country singer-songwriter

The phone rings and it's my girlfriend. She is annoyed with her husband for being cheap. "He is so ridiculous. He told me I have to return the new couch I bought yesterday. He thinks the ten-year-old sofa in the living room is just fine and we don't need to spend the money. Unbelievable!"

I validate her frustration and then ask her to put herself in his shoes. "There is no good reason why we can't spend $900 on a new sofa," she argues, ignoring my suggestion.

We have been friends for years, and she and her partner have been having this same argument for over a decade. She wants to spend; he wants to save. She calls him cheap; he calls her extravagant. This time the conflict is over furniture, but I have heard this same argument over buying a new dishwasher, purchasing concert tickets, and remodeling the basement. You see, their argument, like so many couples' fights, is not about the money. It is really about their different money mindsets.

A money mindset is the sum of all your thoughts and beliefs about money. It is influenced by a variety of factors, including your family money messages, your money personality, and your financial experiences. Here's the tricky part: most of us are not aware that we have a money mindset or how it influences our actions. For example, my girlfriend's money mindset says, "Hard-earned money should be enjoyed." Her husband's money mind-set says, "Money should be saved and only spent when absolutely necessary." Neither of these perspectives is wrong, they're just different. And until this couple identifies the underlying cause of their financial arguments—different money mindsets—they will keep fighting about money.

Individuals, couples, and families spend too much time fighting about dollars and cents, and not enough time trying to understand each other's money mindsets. In other words, it is not about the price of milk, but what motivated you or someone you love to *buy* the milk in the first place that matters.

Think about the last financial disagreement you had with a loved one. How much time did you spend proving to the other person that you were right and they were wrong? Be honest. My guess is it was more time than you invested in figuring out how to put yourself in the other person's shoes so you could comprehend his or her perspective.

Here is a great example from my own marriage. One day I bought a $32 coffeemaker to replace the old, dirty one in the kitchen. I was excited about my purchase, as I had saved a few dollars with a coupon. Notice that my money mindset values thrift and savings. When my husband got home from work, the coffeemaker was in the box on the kitchen table. He looked at me quizzically and said, "We don't need a new coffeemaker, ours is fine." I explained that I got a great deal. He replied, "But we don't need a new coffeemaker. I think you should return it."

"Really? Didn't you just buy a new mountain bike that cost over $1,000?" I fired back. "What is the big deal about spending thirty bucks?"

"I needed the bike, we don't need the appliance," he replied.

"You *needed* the bike?" I asked.

"Yes, my old bike frame cracked and I needed a new bike. But our coffeemaker still works so we don't need a new one."

The conversation went on like this for a good 30 minutes. As I climbed into bed that night, I swore on my grandmother's grave I was not returning the coffeemaker.

A few days went by and the coffeemaker still sat in its box on the kitchen counter. The stubborn kid in me was never giving in. The adult voice shouted, "This is absurd!" As my internal war raged on, Brian seemed to have forgotten the whole incident.

Time passed and I talked to a few friends about the situation before I realized that the argument was not about the money. It was about our diverse money mindsets. Brian was brought up in a family that didn't have much money, so appliances were only replaced when they broke. My family had more resources, and spent money not when things were broken, but when they were on sale. We were both honoring our family money messages. They just happened to conflict with each other. The next day, I returned the coffeemaker.

That night Brian and I discussed my decision to make the return. Instead of butting heads, we listened to each other and laughed about how blown out of proportion this disagreement became. I gained more insight into his money mindset and he did the same with mine. We agreed to try to have this type of discussion the next time we didn't see eye-to-eye financially.

By identifying and talking more about our money mindsets, Brian and I now spend more time finding solutions that work for our family. It is a better use of our energy and ultimately, makes us a more financially savvy couple.

The next time you find yourself and your partner or a loved one disagreeing about money, take a step back and refocus your attention on identifying and discussing your respective money mindsets. In Chapters 5 and 6, I will show you exactly how to do this and how it can help reduce financial tension and increase mutual understanding in your life.

It's All in Your Head

Everyone has a money mindset that is made up of individual thoughts and attitudes about money and its purpose in life. These are called *money scripts*. Like a movie script tells an actor what to say and how to behave in each scene, a money script dictates what you say and how you behave around money in a particular situation. For example, if your money script says "Asking for money is rude," then chances are you find it very difficult to ask a friend for the money she owes you. Not because you don't deserve to be paid back, but because you believe it would be impolite to bring it up. To change the behavior of not talking about money, you need to shift your money script.

Before I show you how to shift unwanted financial habits such as not talking about money with others, let's look at the other factors that influence your unique money mindset. These factors include your family money messages, culture, gender, generation, religious affiliation, socioeconomic status, and personal financial experiences.

Family Money Messages

How your parents and caregivers handled financial matters during your childhood greatly affects your financial decision making as an adult. If your parents fought about money constantly and worked three jobs to make ends meet, you probably considered money scarce and talking about it difficult. However, if you grew up in a family with plenty of resources and your parents talked calmly about money, you may find managing money pleasurable. Or you may have been raised in an affluent home where discussing financial matters outside of the home was strongly discouraged, so you avoid these conversations with your friends. These early childhood experiences, especially those that took place between the ages of 5 and 14, form the majority of your money scripts and influence your financial habits daily.

Because money scripts are primarily formed during childhood, they tend to be overly simplistic and often take the form of all-or-nothing statements. These scripts don't fully appreciate the complexities of making and managing money as an adult today. When left unexamined, these naïve generalizations may cause you to act in childlike ways in adulthood. If you feel like you or your partner act like bratty teenagers when sitting down to pay the bills, it could be that your money mindsets are stuck in adolescence. To further muddle matters, the taboo against talking about money, especially the emotional side of finance, means that most of your money scripts reside in your unconscious mind. This means that your money scripts impact your financial decision making every day, but more often than not, they do so without your consent.

Many of your thoughts and beliefs about money were passed down to you from previous generations. Because talking about money is taboo in most families, these financial legacies probably were not overtly communicated to you. Instead you formed your money mindset based on observations of how your parents, grandparents, and other influential adults interacted with money. And each person in your family may have interpreted these events differently. One sibling may have viewed mom and dad working hard as admirable, while another saw it as shameful. Therefore, you and your siblings can grow up in the same family and have very different money mindsets.

Stanley and Tanya are a good example of this phenomenon. They are siblings who watched their immigrant parents work long hours in the family restaurant. Stanley appreciated his parents' work ethic and grew up to emulate it. His money script is "Hard work pays off." Conversely, Tanya felt embarrassed by her working-class parents and avoided introducing her friends to them. Her money script is "Working hard gets you nowhere." Same family. Different script. Not surprisingly, Stanley took over the restaurant when his father passed away. Tanya married an investment banker and worked in finance until she had kids. Each sibling made financial decisions based on their unique money mindset. Neither choice is right or wrong, but they are vastly different.

Culture

Chances are if you grew up in the United States as a member of the mainstream culture, you received consumer-driven messages such as "the man who dies with the most toys wins" and "spend now, save later." Credit and debit card use is commonplace and being in debt is not unusual. However, if you were born in another country or raised by parents from another culture, you probably received different money messages. For example, in the Hispanic American culture, personal debt is taboo.[1]

Money scripts such as "There is no such thing as good debt" and "Only buy what you can pay for today" may make it difficult for someone with this heritage to take out a mortgage to buy a home, or occasionally use a credit card for larger purchases. In the Asian American culture, investing in higher education is strongly valued and money scripts such as "Education is priceless" may cause parents to forgo a careful cost–benefit analysis of an expensive Ivy League tuition versus a more modest outlay for a community college.[2] In African American culture, money scripts are heavily influenced by centuries of slavery and its negative financial impact. According to Brad Klontz and Ted Klontz, authors of *Mind Over Money*, African Americans are more likely to be "asset poor," and less likely to leave a financial inheritance for the next generation. This translates into many individuals from this culture being pessimistic about their ability to get ahead financially.

Hispanic Americans and Asian Americans often live in multigenerational homes where the expectation is that your financial success should be shared with the extended family. Rianka R. Dorsainvil, CFP®, who is African American and Hispanic, works with many multicultural clients who were the first in their families to go to college. She describes the pressure many feel to financially support their extended family, especially when they start earning a good living. "They look at you as the breadwinner of the family, and the successful child. They also see you as the piggy bank for the family." The family message is "Why can't you help out your auntie, uncle, grandma, mom or dad now that you have a good income?"

According to Dorsainvil, the problem with this cultural money script is it doesn't factor in the individual's need to be financially secure before supporting others. She finds that many of these first-generation college graduates give financial gifts to family members to their own financial detriment. Dorsainvil coaches her clients on how to balance their own financial needs with this strong cultural money message. In her opinion, money silence contributes to the disconnect between family expectations and what a person may actually be capable of giving to their loved ones. If money is not talked about, it becomes harder for you to tell your family that you can't afford to give them money.[3]

A complete review of all the cultural influences on money mindsets is not in the scope of this book. But it is worth noting that the United States is becoming more multicultural every year. Time will tell if this means that cultural money messages shift and blend as our population becomes more integrated, or if they remain distinct to each cultural group.

Gender

As discussed earlier, men and women are often reared with different societal and family money messages. Historically, boys have been raised to be competitive, money-motivated, and "good providers" for the family. Girls have been taught to be good caregivers, emotionally supportive to others, and to put their financial wants and needs second to those around them. When it comes to financial literacy training, some studies suggest that parents talk to their sons more than their daughters about financial goals and investing, thus reinforcing the notion that it's a man's job to make, manage, and invest the family income.[4]

While these traditional gender roles are shifting in the modern family, the money messages associated with gender run deep. I have coached many accomplished women who secretly struggle to ask for a fair wage at work, who won't deposit money into their retirement fund if it means fewer resources for their children, or who put their financial dreams aside to support their partners' dreams.

Janet is a good example of how gender roles can negatively impact a woman's ability to earn and manage money. She is a member of the baby boomer generation who divorced her husband 15 years ago. Janet has a PhD, owns a business, and is a very independent person. However, when it comes to money, she still relies on her ex-husband to make investment decisions. In a coaching session, I asked Janet why she still let her ex-husband control her money. She simply replied, "I was taught by my father that it was a man's duty to take care of his wife financially. I always thought when I remarried I would have my new husband take over my investments. I just haven't fallen in love again."

While it is Janet's prerogative to allow her ex-husband to oversee her investments, her response speaks volumes about her money mindset and her belief in her ability to make wise financial decisions. As the result of our coaching, Janet decided to hire a financial advisor instead of relying on her ex-husband for this advice. This was a big step toward taking control of her finances and being more empowered around money.

It is not just the female money mindset that is influenced by gender. Men's financial attitudes are also affected. The societal belief is that men are supposed to be knowledgeable and enjoy investing. What happens when you're a guy who doesn't like to think about money? You do what Scott does. You marry a woman who is financially savvy and let her manage the money. When I asked Scott, a 44-year-old schoolteacher, about his desire to delegate the couple's money matters to his wife, he admitted that he doesn't feel good about his lack of financial knowledge. One of his main money scripts is "It is too late to learn about finances." The few times he has gone to meet with the couple's advisor, he acted as if he understood investments and the recommendations offered. "The advisor had no idea that I would have preferred to be anywhere but in that appointment." Scott, like many of his male peers, feels pressured to act as if he is financially literate. "It is too embarrassing to admit that I am a guy who doesn't know about this stuff."

Generation

In addition to your cultural background and gender, the challenges and triumphs of your generation color your view of money and wealth. For example, Eleanor, a woman in her late seventies from the traditional generation (those born before 1946), is frugal and likes to defer financial decisions to her husband. She lived through the Great Depression and World War II, and knows what it means to save before you spend. Conversely, her granddaughter Sophie, who is in her early thirties and part of the millennial generation (those born after 1980), uses her debit card to make all her purchases, has a large student loan to pay off, and believes in financial equality when it comes to financial decision making in her marriage. Neither approach is wrong. Each woman's money mindset is informed by her generational experience and impacts how she thinks and feels about money and financial decision making.

Table 4.1 offers a chart highlighting some of the key influencers, traits, and financial concerns of the traditional, baby boom, generation X, and millennial generations.

When you and your loved ones discuss money matters as a family, it's important to be aware of and appreciate generational differences. Instead of seeing other generations as the enemy, embrace the strengths of each one. For example, if Eleanor and Sophie meet, it may be best for Eleanor to understand Sophie's need as a millennial to be asked for her input. Sophie needs to appreciate her traditional grandmother's need to find a frugal solution. It may just turn out that Sophie knows of an iPhone application that can save her grandmother some money.

Table 4.1   Generational Differences and Money Mindsets

Generation	Birth Year	Key Influences	Traits	$ Mindset
Traditional	Before 1946	Automobile Great Depression World War II	Loyal Patriotic Frugal Respectful	Save then Spend
Baby Boomer	1947–1964	Civil/Women's Rights Moon Landing Watergate	Competitive Idealistic Spenders Optimistic	Financially Sandwiched In
Gen X	1965–1979	Latchkey Kids Personal Computer 24-hour Media	Entrepreneurial Skeptical Independent Pay with Credit	DIY Finances
Millennial	1980–2000	September 11th Social Media The Great Recession	Collaborative Socially Aware Charitable Tech Savvy	Fiscally Conservative

Religion

Religion is another major influence on a person's money mindset. Religion and money have an interesting, sometimes strained relationship. No matter what your religious upbringing or current affiliation, religion usually has a bearing on your money scripts. For example, the biblical scripture that states "The *love of* money is the root of all evil" has had a powerful effect on Christians and how they view wealth versus poverty. In Christianity, it is noble to be poor. Another scripture cautions, "It is easier for a camel to go through the eye of a needle than a rich man to enter into the Kingdom of God."[5] The clear message is that being wealthy makes it very hard for you to be a good Christian.

Having been raised Irish Catholic, I can tell you firsthand how these early teachings influenced my career choices and my ability to tolerate financial success. When I graduated from college, I felt like I was paid too much for working as an FDIC bank examiner, and eventually left to work in the nonprofit sector. As a result, for 15 years I was an under-earner. I did good work and found it satisfying, but without my husband's income I would have lived at just above the poverty level. After years of coaching, I finally realized that it was okay to enjoy work, to be adequately compensated, and to live free of constant internal conflict around my worth.

Subsequently, I have coached others with Christian upbringings and found they struggled with similar money scripts. However, some religions celebrate wealth and embrace it. My friend Beth, who I mentioned in the introduction, comes from a tight-knit Jewish family. In Judaism, the accumulation of wealth is not viewed as evil so long as wealth is used wisely. This is summed up in the Yiddish proverb that states, "With money in your pocket, you are wise and you are handsome and you sing well, too." Beth is generous with her resources and always looking out for others in need. When asked, she is quick to tell me she was raised in a family where you showed your love and support by giving your financial resources freely. When we initially talked about money, I found this perspective both surprising and enlightening. For the first time, I realized I didn't have to feel bad about money.

In Buddhism, wealth is temporary and not a path to happiness. Buddhists don't see money as evil, and instead view it as a way to empower others. According to Ethan Nichtern, a prominent Buddhist teacher and author of *The Road Home*, "Money can also be spiritual or divine, by powering whatever positive activity you want to engage in."[6] In other words, you can be rich and a good person.

Religion is about more than money, of course, and it serves an important purpose in many peoples' lives. But when it comes to examining your money mindset, it is helpful to look at the financial messages embedded in the spiritual teachings you grew up with or follow now. You may initially feel that religion and money are two separate entities. However, in my experience as a coach and educator, the impact of your religious upbringing on your money mindset is often unspoken but powerful, and thus an area worth exploring.

Socioeconomic Status

The socioeconomic status of your family of origin also contributes to how you think and feel about money. If you grew up in a lower socioeconomic class, you probably have different money scripts than those who were raised in a financially privileged home. Those from impoverished backgrounds tend to have money scripts based on a scarcity mindset, such as "There will never be enough money," or "Wealthy people got that way by taking advantage of people like us." The result is many of these individuals feel disempowered to change their financial situations.[7]

But the grass is not greener on the other side, since individuals from affluent families have problematic money scripts as well. While financial resources are abundant, there is a fear of losing wealth or being judged for having it. Those who are born into affluence can fall into the trap of confusing their net worth with their self-worth, and have trouble finding a meaningful purpose in life. Common money scripts include "I will never buy anything unless it is new," and "You should never tell others what you have." These money scripts can fuel an unhealthy self-image and make talking about money challenging.[8] While many think being born rich or well-off makes breaking money silence easier, wealth often actually makes it tougher.

Christopher and Julie didn't realize how much their socioeconomic status influenced their money mindsets until Julie's family sold their business and she inherited almost 10 million dollars. At first the couple experienced their new wealth as a wonderful gift—until they started fighting about money. By the time they met with me, Christopher had run up a huge credit card debt and Julie was contemplating divorce. In our first meeting, I asked them about their money histories. Christopher had grown up in a poor neighborhood with a single mom who often mismanaged money. His money script, once they inherited the money, was "We are lucky to have inherited the money and we should enjoy it." Conversely, Julie was raised in an upper-middle-class home with two parents and three siblings. She was taught to save money, and to not take her family's financial situation for granted. Her money script, once they inherited the money, was "My parents worked hard so I could inherit this money, so I need to preserve it." Their money mindsets were the root of many of their arguments. With coaching, they learned how to talk about their diverse viewpoints and how the socioeconomic environments they were raised in impacted their beliefs about how to use their inheritance.

Personal Financial Experiences

In addition to all the factors listed above, your money scripts are also impacted by your own personal money experiences. Significant events such as winning the lottery, receiving a sizable inheritance, filing for bankruptcy, going through an expensive divorce, or being laid off all leave a lasting mark on your money psyche and, ultimately, alter your financial belief system. Each of these events comes with a variety of mixed emotions that need to be understood and eventually integrated into your money mindsets.

My friend Cheryl credits her divorce with helping her become more mindful about money. When she was married, she spent money without thinking, knowing her husband's six-figure salary would cover the bills. When he left her for a younger woman, she was forced to live on a fixed income for the first time in her life. "At first, I hated it. But over time I learned how to create a budget and stick with it. Now, I actually feel really proud of myself when I balance my checkbook and see that my spending is on track."

My money mindset was changed forever when the contractor I mentioned in the introduction swindled my husband and me out of thousands of dollars. Prior to this experience, I would have sworn on my mother's grave that good people always have money in the bank and only irresponsible people fall behind on their bills. However, after our contractor walked away with our hard-earned cash and I couldn't keep current on our household bills, I realized being a good person had nothing to do with your savings account balance or your bill's past-due status. While this was a painful lesson to learn, it taught me how to have a healthier, more adult relationship with money. It also was the precursor to starting my company, KBK Wealth Connection, so I could help others understand their money psychology. This traumatic financial event changed my life forever, for the better.

Your money mindset is like your fingerprint. It is unique to you. You may share some money scripts with family members, or others with similar cultural, socioeconomic, and personal experiences, but ultimately *you* are the only person with *your* mindset. It is up to you to identify your money scripts and communicate these attitudes to those you love. The benefit is that doing so increases mutual understanding, and reduces financial tension.

At the end of the chapter, you will complete an exercise aimed at identifying some of your money scripts. For now, let's look at how you can change your money mindset.

Changing Your Money Mindset

The connection between money and emotion is real. It makes finance and investing interesting. It also complicates talking about money with loved ones. Dare I say that the emotional side of money is the cause for money silence? It is our society's discomfort with feelings and conflict that keeps us quiet. It is the financial industry's reluctance to address the human side of finance that stops your advisor from proactively helping you to engage in healthy money talk with your partner and your family. It is the overall false premise that if you have all your ducks in a row, then you won't have anxiety, fear, excitement, joy, or worry about your financial future. That somehow, you are bad if you are not logical about money.

It is time to let go of the idea that you should always be rational about money. Instead, embrace the notion that your thoughts and feelings about money impact your actions, and ultimately your habits. If you do this, then you can change your behaviors simply by identifying and changing the thoughts you have about them.

Here is how it typically works (see Figure 4.1). A financial situation arises. You have an automatic thought or money script about the situation. Based on your money script, you then experience an automatic feeling that in turn, triggers an automatic behavior. This chain of events happens almost simultaneously in your unconscious mind. You then decide how to act based on this data. Because this entire sequence happens quickly and unconsciously, it appears to be something that you cannot control. However, if you identify your money scripts, you can change your feelings and your behaviors, and ultimately the financial outcome.

Jen is a good example of how emotions can impact financial habits and turn what is rationally viewed as a good behavior into an unhealthy one. As a child, Jen received a weekly allowance from her parents. Every week she took great pride in filling out her deposit slip and putting the money in her savings account. Jen loved the bank and the way the tellers would treat her as an adult during each transaction. On the way home, her dad would always ask if she wanted to buy anything with her allowance like a

Figure 4.1: The Connection Between Your Money Scripts, Feelings and Behaviors

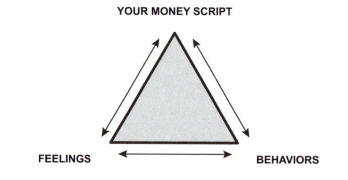

toy or some penny candy. Jennifer would shake her head "no" and her dad would exclaim, "What a good little saver you are!" This series of events played out over and over again, and her thoughts, feelings, and behaviors were always the same. Eventually, Jen developed the money scripts "It feels good to save," and "People (her dad, the bank tellers) like me when I save money."

While saving is a healthy financial practice, being able to spend money is also part of a well-balanced financial life. By the time I met Jen, she was 32 and had a great deal of trouble buying anything she viewed as not necessary. She was so restrictive in her spending that she did not own a box spring or frame for her bed, because in her mind, she could simply sleep on the mattress on the floor. She made a large salary as a physician's assistant, but did not allow herself any monetary joy. In fact, she denied herself all the pleasures that come with being single in a city and working in a large hospital. She declined social invitations, as going out to eat was costly, and she missed out on many other opportunities for the same reason.

Jen knew something was wrong with her relationship with money. Her extreme saving habits were making her miserable, even though other people admired her self-restraint. She eventually decided to reach out for help and we began working together. The first week I taught her that money decisions are not always rational and how to identify her automatic thoughts, feelings, and behaviors around savings using the Mind Over Money method (or MOM for short). Below are the steps of the MOM method and what Jen discovered in her first appointment.

The Mind Over Money Method

Step 1: Identify the problematic situation.

> *I have an inability to spend any money on myself and that makes me unhappy and lonely.*

Step 2: What automatic thoughts (money scripts) do you experience in this situation?

> *Money should be saved. It is bad to spend. I will get out of control if I start spending on myself. Saving money is a good practice.*

Step 3: What automatic feelings do you experience when you have these automatic thoughts?

> *I feel fear, anxiety, and shame.*

Step 4: What automatic behaviors do you experience in this situation?

My heart races and I get sweaty palms.

Step 5: What is the automatic outcome, or the financial decision you make?

I don't spend the money. Initially I feel proud. Later I feel depressed and deprived.

Step 6: Test each money script to see if it is a rational fact or an individual belief. (A word of caution: Money beliefs run deep and sometimes feel factual when they are really just beliefs.)

"Money always should be saved."—Belief, as this statement is too black-and-white to always be true.

"It is bad to spend."—Belief, as this statement is full of negative self-judgment.

"I will get out of control."—Belief, as you don't know the future.

"Saving is a good practice."—Fact, as it is not a self-judgment but a healthy financial practice when done in moderation.

Step 7: Challenge all the beliefs or money scripts listed in Step 6 by identifying other ways of thinking about the same situation.

"Money should be saved" is an all-or-nothing statement that is not always accurate. Sometimes you need to spend money.

"It is bad to spend" is also an all-or-nothing statement that is not necessarily true. Spending money is part of a healthy relationship with money and can be a wise financial habit.

"I will get out of control" is a fear that I have but not a fact. I have never gotten out of control with money. I may be uncomfortable and worry that one purchase will lead to overspending, but there is no evidence to support this. Besides, I have time to ask for help before my spending becomes a problem.

Step 8: Reframe the money scripts in Step 7 to be more accurate given your adult life situation.

New money script: "Saving and spending money is part of the ebb and flow of life and I deserve to take care of myself by both having a savings account for the future and having a spending allowance for buying non-essential items and having fun in the here and now."

Notice how Jen's new money script is less childlike and more in line with how an adult needs to use money to live a balanced, healthy lifestyle.

Step 9: What impact do these reframed money scripts have on your feelings and behaviors?

I feel less anxious and fearful. I don't feel ashamed.

The intensity of Jen's original feelings declined. While she still felt anxious and fearful, her shame dissipated. Overall, these reframed money scripts made her feel calmer and more in control.

Step 10: How can you remember these reframed money scripts when faced with a similar situation?

I can carry them with me, and I can post them on my refrigerator as a reminder.

I encouraged Jen to write down the reframed money scripts on an index card and carry the card in her purse. This way when she was faced with a similar situation, she could re-read these new money scripts and in turn, start the process of replacing her unhealthy thoughts with healthier ones.

While Jen's money scripts and habits were firmly entrenched and required longer-term coaching, she eventually mastered the MOM method and could use this technique to quickly adjust her perspective when she faced a spending decision (see Figure 4.2).

Eventually, Jen bought herself a bedroom set and worked with a financial planner to determine how much disposable income she had to work with each month. She became less isolated, started going out more with friends, and found that embracing money as something that ebbs and flows allowed her to be more flexible in other areas of her life as well.

Figure 4.2: The Connection Between Jen's Money Script, Feelings and Behaviors

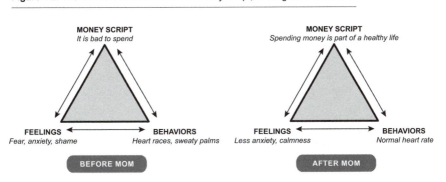

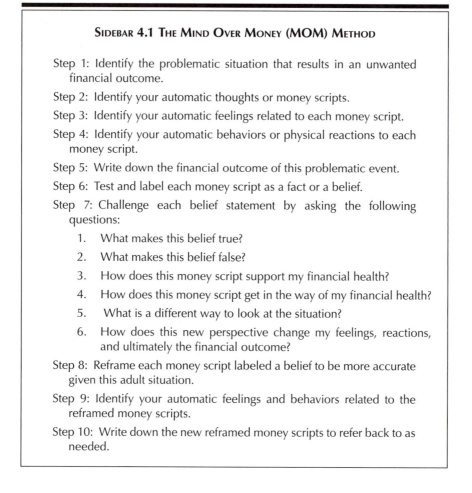

SIDEBAR 4.1 THE MIND OVER MONEY (MOM) METHOD

Step 1: Identify the problematic situation that results in an unwanted financial outcome.

Step 2: Identify your automatic thoughts or money scripts.

Step 3: Identify your automatic feelings related to each money script.

Step 4: Identify your automatic behaviors or physical reactions to each money script.

Step 5: Write down the financial outcome of this problematic event.

Step 6: Test and label each money script as a fact or a belief.

Step 7: Challenge each belief statement by asking the following questions:

   1.   What makes this belief true?
   2.   What makes this belief false?
   3.   How does this money script support my financial health?
   4.   How does this money script get in the way of my financial health?
   5.   What is a different way to look at the situation?
   6.   How does this new perspective change my feelings, reactions, and ultimately the financial outcome?

Step 8: Reframe each money script labeled a belief to be more accurate given this adult situation.

Step 9: Identify your automatic feelings and behaviors related to the reframed money scripts.

Step 10: Write down the new reframed money scripts to refer back to as needed.

Change the Conversation

Discussing money mindsets changes the conversation. This technique can be very helpful when two people don't see eye-to-eye on a financial matter. Instead of trying to place blame or fighting over who is right and who is wrong in a particular situation, it allows two people to work toward mutual understanding. You may not agree by the end of the discussion, but at least you will have some insight into why your partner, parent, or child is acting a certain way. Understanding where another person is coming from makes it easier to find common ground and work toward a resolution.

Sierra and her husband are a great example of how talking about money mindsets reduces tension and helps partners discuss money matters more effectively. Sierra works in the financial industry and has an in-depth understanding of the stock market and investments. Her husband works in music copyrighting and was born in England. He typically shies away from dealing with money. He is less financially literate, and in Sierra's opinion, he abdicates his financial responsibilities too often. This leads Sierra to become frustrated, as she doesn't want to manage the family finances and make all the investment decisions alone. They often fight after seeing their advisor.

"If we try to talk about how much we've got invested, what we want to invest, and where the money is allocated, we usually get into an argument," Sierra says. "My husband and I grew up in completely different ways. Our diverse backgrounds have had an incredible impact on how we communicate about money as a couple."

At the recommendation of the couple's financial advisor, Sierra and her husband started talking less about the technical aspects of investing and more about their money histories, money mindsets, and vision for the future. By doing so, the couple started to engage in more satisfying and productive dialogues. "I just had this conversation recently where I asked my husband a series of questions about the future and what he wanted for our son. And the more I got him thinking about the future, the more we were able to come together as a couple on what we needed to do financially to accomplish this vision."

Sierra also did something that is vital in every money talk. She got curious about the other person's experience. She stopped judging her partner for his upbringing and his family money messages. Instead, Sierra asked a series of open-ended questions and tried to put herself in her husband's shoes. This approach reduced her husband's defensiveness and allowed him to talk more openly about money with her.

In Chapter 6, you will learn how curiosity is a key element for engaging in a productive money talk and how you can tap into your natural sense of wonder about the world around you.

Summary

In this chapter, you learned how your thoughts, feelings, and beliefs about money impact your financial habits. Let's review the key points.

- Identifying your money mindset can help you change your behaviors and conversations.

- Many factors contribute to the development of your money mindset (family money messages, culture, gender, generation, religion, socioeconomic status, and personal financial experiences).

- Your emotions can and do influence your financial decisions.

- As an adult you can shift your money mindset using a tool called Mind Over Money (MOM).

- If you invest the time in understanding your money mindset and then inspire others to do the same, money talk becomes much easier and more enjoyable.

Money Talk Challenge: Identifying Your Money Mindset

Complete the following sentences with the first thought that comes into your mind. Do not censor your responses or worry whether your answers are politically correct. The only goal of this exercise is to help you bring your unconscious money scripts into your conscious thought.

1. Money is . . .
2. Wealthy people are . . .
3. Poor people are . . .
4. My mother taught me money was . . .
5. My father taught me money was . . .
6. My grandmother taught me money was . . .
7. My grandfather taught me money was . . .
8. Saving money is . . .
9. Spending money is. . .
10. Investing money is . . .
11. Giving money to others is . . .
12. Talking about money is . . .
13. Asking people for money is . . .
14. People who talk about money are . . .
15. When a loved one talks about money, I . . .

Take a moment to review your answers and consider how each one impacts your current spending, saving, investing, and charitable giving habits. Notice any trends or themes. Select one money script you would like to change. Use the MOM method described in this chapter to examine that automatic thought. Write down what you learned about yourself after completing this process.

Your money mindset is made up hundreds of money scripts, so it will take time for you to uncover all of your beliefs. However, completing this Money Talk Challenge will make it easier to bring these formerly unconscious thoughts into conscious awareness so you can change them if you want to.

For Advisors

Advisors are people too! It is important that you complete the Money Talk Challenge above and consider how your money mindset impacts your work with clients. Once you have completed this first step, answer the following questions.

1. How does your money mindset color the questions you ask clients during the discovery process and during regular meetings?
2. How does your money mindset influence the recommendations you give to your clients?
3. How might your money mindset impact the type of clients you prefer working with?
4. How might you use the money mindset identification exercise and the MOM method to help your clients going forward?
5. What else did you learn from this activity that you will use to grow your practice?

CHAPTER FIVE

The Buck Stops Here: Dare to Break the Silence

Ten percent of conflicts are due to difference in opinion. Ninety percent are due to wrong tone of voice.

—Unknown

Do you remember the George and Ira Gershwin song, "Let's Call the Whole Thing Off," famously performed by Fred Astaire and Ginger Rogers in the 1937 film *Shall We Dance*? If you like old movies or you are from the traditional generation you just might. If not, then here are some of the lyrics:

> You like potato and I like potahto
> You like tomato and I like tomahto
> Potato, potahto, Tomato, tomahto.
> Let's call the whole thing off

These lyrics capture the frustration, and sometimes silliness, of partners seeing life from opposing angles. The fact that this happens in your relationships makes you human. It is what you do about it, especially when it comes to money, that is important.

This is where identifying and communicating your money mindsets really matters. Whether it is with your spouse, business partner, or parent, talking openly about money is the key to healthier relationships. It is your choice. You can stay stuck in the same argument or even paralyzed in silence. Or you can start talking about the underlying money beliefs that cause financial tension in your life.

In this chapter, I will focus on money talk between romantic partners. Know that most, if not all of these techniques also apply to other relationships. If you are not married or currently dating, read this chapter with an important loved one in mind. This may be a parent, child, or sibling. Later on in Chapters 8 and 9, I will go into greater detail on specific tactics to use when engaging in money talk with children and parents.

Remember the couple at the beginning of Chapter 4 who were fighting about buying a new sofa? They have recently learned how to identify and share their money scripts with each other. While they still don't agree on all purchases, the number of calls I get from my girlfriend complaining about her "cheap" husband has definitely decreased. The key to their success has been talking about their money attitudes, and not just fighting over dollars and cents. This couple still disagrees from time to time, but now they accept that having different viewpoints will make them financially stronger as a couple.

Money Compatibility

It is a sad fact that most couples don't find out if they are financially compatible until they are living together or married. The exception to this rule tends to be people who are in their second marriages, as they generally have experienced the pain that comes with being in a relationship where money is a source of conflict. So, whether you are married, living together, or dating, it is important to find out if you and your partner are financially well matched. If you are money-compatible, then your financial life won't be perfect but it will be less rocky. If you are not well-suited for each other, then you can decide to roll up your sleeves and work on this part of your relationship. Or if you are like Hannah, you can decide to go your separate ways before the relationship gets too serious.

Hannah had dated Andrew for six months. When they first began dating, he wined and dined her at nice restaurants in the city. But once they started seeing each other exclusively, something changed. Hannah told me, "He became really cheap. If I wanted to go out for a drink after work, he would insist we meet at his apartment for a beer. I understand the need to save money, but over time it just seemed to get worse. The final straw was when he got angry with me for buying an expensive shampoo for myself—and we didn't even live together. I told him it was none of his business what I spent on shampoo." She described the fight that ensued. Her position was that she worked hard and had a right to buy any type of shampoo she liked. Andrew thought that purchasing a luxury brand of

shampoo was unnecessary and that Hannah should save money by buying a drugstore brand. "I can't believe I broke up with a guy over a bottle
of shampoo, but I did. I just didn't want to spend my life with someone
who thought he could tell me how to spend my own money!"

While Hannah laughs about it now, the story speaks volumes about
money compatibility. Andrew's money mindset was not wrong, but it
was dramatically different from Hannah's. They simply were not a good
financial fit. While she valued simple luxuries such as special soaps and
shampoos, she also saved money in other ways. Andrew felt that forgoing daily treats was the best way to save for the future. He also believed
that as the man in the relationship, he should call the financial shots.
Hannah did not agree. Eventually, she dated and married a man who
didn't care if she bought designer-brand shampoo or not. "It's not perfect when it comes to money, but our values and financial habits are
more closely in line."

Money compatibility is defined as having similar financial goals and
values, and an ability to discuss and resolve financial differences. Money
compatibility does not mean that you both have the same money mindset, or that you always agree about how to use your wealth. But it does
require you to be like-minded when it comes to your short-term and long-
term financial vision.

Steve and Warren are a good example of a money-compatible couple.
Steve is very conservative in his spending and rarely splurges on dining
out or clothes. While Warren enjoys fine wine and going out with his
friends, he too likes being thrifty. He clips coupons, looks for discounts
and sales, and does a good job of keeping to the budget that Steve has
established for the family. They both love to travel and use the money
they save on day-to-day expenses to take one or two exotic vacations a
year. Of course, they financially disagree from time to time, but for the
most part they are very well-suited.

Conversely, David and Zoe are a good example of a money-incompati-
ble couple. David works for a start-up technology company and likes to
make and spend a lot of money. He works long hours at the office and
believes that he deserves to be rewarded. He considers his vintage car collection his reward for being a good provider for his family. His wife Zoe
sees things differently. She resents David's long hours at work and thinks
the car collection is a waste of money. Zoe likes to hike, knit, and read.
She rarely goes shopping for herself and is embarrassed by her husband's
showy lifestyle. Their values are just very different. As a result, they fight
about money often and are considering separation.

As these couples exemplify, shared values are important when it comes to financial compatibility. Whether you realize it or not, how you spend and save money often comes down to what you think is important in life— in other words, what you value. An easy way to find out more about how you use money to express your values is to look at your most recent credit card statement or bank statement. Review each entry and identify what value you were honoring by spending money in this way. For example, if you have three credit card charges for the Barnes and Noble bookstore, you probably value reading. Or if you have two debit entries for Ron's Bike Shop, then you most likely value exercise in the form of biking. When partners are compatible they usually value and invest in similar things.

In addition to being money-compatible, it is important to be financially fit. A financially fit couple is one that has the desire and financial know- how to proactively plan for their future. These couples tend to work with professional advisors and are more likely to talk about their finances, because they see this as a vital part of the planning process.

Let's take a minute to find out how financially fit you and your partner are. Take this brief quiz to identify your strengths as a couple and the areas you may want to improve.

How Financially Fit Are You and Your Partner?

For each statement below, indicate if you always (A) engage in this behavior, sometimes (S) engage in this behavior, or never (N) engage in this behavior.

_____ 1. As a couple, we talk about money regularly (no less than once a month).

_____ 2. We know each other's financial strengths and challenges and try to focus on each other's strengths.

_____ 3. We work as a team, capitalizing on each other's strong suits to make, manage, and invest our financial resources to the best of our abilities.

_____ 4. We financially disagree from time and time and know how to resolve these conflicts.

_____ 5. Both of us have a basic understanding of where our money is invested and how these investments support our future financial plans.

_____ 6. We occasionally hide purchases from each other to avoid fighting about money.

_____ 7. We spend, save, invest, and gift money according to our shared and individual life values.

_____ 8. We proactively talk to our children or the next generation about money.

_____ 9. We have an estate plan and have talked with each other about our end-of-life wishes.

_____ 10. We have a spending plan and communicate with each other when one of us wants go outside these parameters.

Now score your answers by assigning the following points and adding up the total number of points you received.

Give yourself 3 points for every Always answer, except on question 6.

Give yourself 0 points for an Always answer on number 6.

Give yourself 1 point for every Sometimes answer.

Give yourself 0 points for every Never answer, except on question 6.

Give yourself 3 points for a Never answer on question 6.

Add up your total points and put that number here_____.

If you scored between 21 and 30 points, congratulations! You are a financially fit couple. You communicate regularly about money matters and are building a solid financial foundation for your family. Keep up the good work by keeping the lines of communication open.

If you scored between 11 and 20 points, good job! You are well on your way to becoming a financially fit couple. You have done a good job addressing some areas of your financial lives and you just need to continue on this path.

If you scored 10 points or less, your financial fitness needs improvement. Use this quiz to help you identify areas to work on. Commit to investing time in working together to improve your score. Also considering hiring a money coach, counselor, or financial advisor to help.

Now that you have learned about money compatibility and financially fit couples, let's look at how myths about conflict prevent many partners from openly and honestly discussing money matters.

"Winner Takes All" and Other Myths about Conflict

In Chapter 1, I discussed the origins of money taboo and how it is perpetuated in society, based on such money myths, as "it is rude and unnecessary to talk about money." In addition to money myths, our society's fear of conflict, especially around financial matters, also fuels money silence. The fallacy is that if we discuss money matters with a romantic partner, a nasty fight will ensue. Recognize any of these excuses?

- "My husband is happier when I don't tell him how much I spent at the spa."
- "My boyfriend is so sensitive about his daughter that I can't talk to him about asking her to pay rent while she lives with us."
- "I don't want to ruin his day off by discussing the cost of my mother's home healthcare this month."

The list goes on and on. These statements feel very true but they often go untested. We think these thoughts; therefore, they must be accurate. The truth is you never know if what you are thinking about money is actually true until you test it out by asking the other person. Yes, talking about money is exactly what you need to do if you are going to find out if you and another person have conflicting views.

Don't get me wrong. I know the money scripts that make up your money mindset feel very real to you. I understand that the idea of discussing and possibly fighting over money matters with your partner can be scary and uncomfortable. But the truth is you will never know the outcome of a financial conversation until you have it. Yes, conflict could happen. But so could mutual understanding and an increase in intimacy. Surprised? Yes, talking about money with a loved one can, and often does, bring you closer.

When Art and Ellen married, each for the second time, they made a conscious decision to manage their money together. Art is a physician with a busy schedule and the primary breadwinner in the family. Ellen supports him by organizing his personal and professional life. She attends all the meetings alongside Art, including appointments with the CPA, the attorney, and their financial advisor. Both partners agreed that in their marriage there would be no financial secrets. Even if they disagree about finances, they talk about it.

As their financial advisor notes, "Art and Ellen have a willingness to communicate on all financial matters, even when they don't see eye-to-eye. This has led to a wonderful successful second marriage and will ultimately lead to a delightful retirement."[1] Yes, talking about money openly and honestly brought Arthur and Ellen closer and it can do the same for you in your partnership.

What are the typical myths that prevent partners from breaking money silence in their lives? In my experience, here are the top three fallacies and how each myth might impact your willingness to engage in a money talk.

Myth 1: Conflict Is a Game with a Winner and Loser

My husband and I used to ski with a couple that fought about everything. They fought about what restaurant to eat at. They argued about what ski trail was the best to traverse. And of course, they disagreed about money. Individually they were good people, but hanging out with them together felt like you were constantly watching a boxing match. Each partner was committed to winning at all costs. In the end, they divorced and neither partner won. Unfortunately, they never learned the truth about conflict.

Contrary to what you may have been told, there is not a winner or a loser in a conflict. There are just two people with diverse viewpoints. One person's perspective is not better or worse than the other person's viewpoint. It is just different. In a healthy disagreement, the focus is not on winning the fight but understanding each partner's thoughts and beliefs about the matter.

When it comes to money talk, understanding your partner's money mindset is the key to a healthy resolution. If you are competitive and like to win, use those skills on the golf course where they are more appropriate. Then jump into your next financial disagreement with the goal of learning more about your partner, not beating him or her in some imaginary contest.

Myth 2: Conflict Is Bad and Should Be Avoided at All Costs

My parents were the opposite of the couple described above. They avoided overt conflict as they were taught that fighting was a bad thing. Any time they would fight, it would be very quiet in the house. My mom would stop talking to my dad and my dad would act as if everything was fine. As an intuitive child, I always sensed when something was amiss but found it very confusing when both my parents would deny what was happening. At times, I wished they would duke it out instead of letting it quietly fester. But they never did.

As an adult I now understand how conflict-avoidant both my parents were and how they thought they were doing the right thing for our family. They were married 54 years, and to the outside world, they appeared to be the perfect couple. But when it came to appreciating and resolving differences, they just didn't have the skills. I can't help but imagine how my relationship with my family may have been different, and more intimate, had my mom and dad been better role models of healthy conflict resolution.

The truth is that conflict in any relationship is healthy. It allows partners to negotiate and set boundaries, it enables them to collaboratively problem-solve, and it deepens the sense of intimacy in a marriage or committed relationship. Talking about and sometimes disagreeing about money is normal and natural. These disagreements allow you and your partner to discuss and appreciate your similarities, and celebrate your differences. If you have children, showing them that you can disagree financially is a good skill to model. It is a lesson that will serve the next generation well.

Myth 3: Conflict Skills Are Innate

In college, I had a girlfriend who bragged that she was good at conflict. "I don't have any problem fighting. I just tell people where to go." As you can imagine, my friend spent her college years arguing with her teachers and her peers. Like many people, she confused her ability to fight with having good conflict resolution skills. While voicing your opinion is an important skill to develop, it is vital that you learn when, where, and how to speak up. To date, my college friend has not mastered this skill!

I don't think it was a coincidence that I gravitated toward her in college. Secretly, I wished I could fight like her. In my twenties, I avoided conflict and had trouble communicating my true feelings if it might upset the other person. I used to think, "oh, if only I had been born with these skills!"

In the end, we were both mistaken. Conflict skills are not innate. You are not born with them. You learn them by witnessing your parents and other influential adults disagree. In my friend's case, her parents fought all the time but didn't resolve their underlying conflicts. In my situation, my parents brushed all their conflicts under the rug. It seems both of us needed to learn conflict resolution skills as adults.

If you do a quick Google search for the term "conflict management courses," you will receive over 3,140,000 hits. The sheer volume of these training courses indicates the large demand for this type of training. Having worked as a psychotherapist for over 15 years and a wealth psychology expert for another 10 years, I can tell you firsthand that most adults struggle to some degree in this area.

The fact that conflict is a part of everyone's financial life, is healthy in a relationship, and is a learned skill may be news to you. Or you may know this intellectually but feel emotionally reluctant to engage in conflict. Either way, understanding where your beliefs about conflict stem from is helpful in changing how you view financial disagreements going forward.

Take a minute to think back to your childhood. Was conflict encouraged or discouraged? When someone in your family was having a disagreement, how did you know these two people were not getting along? Did they avoid each other? Did they yell and scream? Did they talk behind each other's back trying to elicit support from other family members? Or did they do something else? Your answers to these questions provide valuable insight into how you approach conflict. As an adult, you have the power to change your outlook and become more open to discussing differences in a new way. At the end of the chapter, the Money Talk Challenge will give you a chance to explore how your conflict mindset influences your willingness and ability to talk openly about money with loved ones.

One of the things that make financial conversations and conflict less anxiety provoking is learning how to fight fair. So, let's look at some guidelines for engaging in healthy money talk.

"The Kingsbury Rules" for Fighting Fair Financially

In the sport of boxing, there is a code of conduct called the Queensbury Rules, written by John Graham Chambers, named after the ninth Marquis of Queensbury, and published in 1867. These rules were created, and later amended, to make sure that boxers were protected from undue harm and the matches were fair.[2] The modern-day version prohibits hitting below the belt, holding, or kicking. These are all useful guidelines that make boxing as safe as it can be—for a contact sport!

Unfortunately, there are no such universally accepted rules for financial fights, but I think there should be. It would help each partner feel safe and make sure that neither partner gets too carried away. To fill this gap, I propose the following "Kingsbury Rules of Fighting Fair Financially." These seven general guidelines provide a framework for healthy money talk.

Take time to review them individually, and then share them with your partner. Some of these rules may be easier for you to comply with than others. Just know that some rules might seem like a no-brainer to you, but may be challenging for your partner to master, and vice versa. Be patient with yourself and your partner as you learn these guidelines and practice talking more openly about money. Like it or not, change takes time.

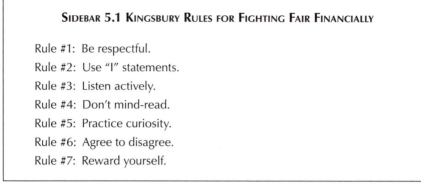

SIDEBAR 5.1 KINGSBURY RULES FOR FIGHTING FAIR FINANCIALLY

Rule #1: Be respectful.
Rule #2: Use "I" statements.
Rule #3: Listen actively.
Rule #4: Don't mind-read.
Rule #5: Practice curiosity.
Rule #6: Agree to disagree.
Rule #7: Reward yourself.

Kingsbury Rule #1: Be Respectful

It is always important to treat the other person in the conversation with respect. Respectful behaviors include listening carefully, not interrupting, and refraining from using profanity or blaming language. Most people want to treat their loved ones with respect but find it becomes harder to do when emotions run high. McKenzie, a wife and caretaker of her husband's elderly mother, explained, "When we are discussing the cost of his mother's care, I start off calm. But the minute I feel like he doesn't appreciate the time it takes to care for her, I snap and say something I regret later. It is hard to be respectful when the topic is so emotional."

Being respectful during a money conversation sounds simple, but it can get complicated when strong feelings emerge or difficult family dynamics are triggered. Take a few deep breaths if you find yourself getting hotheaded. If that doesn't work, take a break from the conversation. Now, when McKenzie starts feeling annoyed talking to her husband, she takes one or two deep breaths to calm down. When that doesn't work, she asks her husband for a time-out. "We actually have laughed a few times during recent meetings. It's much better than it used to be."

It is okay to take a break from a money conversation when either or both of you get emotionally overwhelmed. But it is important that you make a plan for when you will continue the dialogue. Based on the situation, decide whether you need five minutes or five days before picking up the conversation where you left off. The amount of time you need may vary, which is fine. Just make sure that you revisit the conversation, as it can be easy to let money silence sneak back in.

Kingsbury Rule #2: Use "I" Statements

Whenever possible, use "I" statements to communicate how you feel and what specific action triggered this emotion. Avoid the urge to point a finger and blame your partner. This allows you to more effectively communicate your message and engage in a more productive conversation. Just look at the difference between these two statements:

Statement 1: "You better stop giving Zachary the gas credit card to fill up his car's gas tank if you ever want him to learn the value of a dollar."

Statement 2: "When I see you giving Zachary the gas credit card to fill up his car's gas tank, I worry that he is not learning the value of a dollar."

The first statement puts the listener on the defensive and has a blaming tone. The second statement identifies the speaker's concerns, her feelings about the specific behavior mentioned, and sets a more positive tone. While these two people may still disagree about how to teach their son the value of a dollar, the likelihood of them calmly discussing their differences is greatly increased by the use of "I" statements.

It takes practice to communicate using "I" statements, especially if you were raised in a family where blame was tossed around like a beach ball. Be patient with yourself and others when you notice the tendency to point a finger. When in doubt use this formula for communicating your concern: *When you (specific behavior), I feel (specific emotion)*. After you state the problematic behavior and the feeling the behavior elicits, you can suggest a new behavior. Your partner can agree or disagree with your recommendation. Either way, this is a much better way to begin the dialogue if conflict resolution is your goal.

Kingsbury Rule #3: Listen Actively

Active listening is a communication technique that aids in mutual understanding. It involves asking open-ended questions, then listening carefully to the answers. Unlike passive listening, active listening involves paying attention to both verbal and nonverbal communication. This type of listening does not involve you offering your opinion on the information your partner shared. Instead, the goal is to try to put yourself in your partner's shoes so you can truly comprehend their perspective.

Active listening sounds simple, but it takes time to learn and master. The following is a formula for active listening. If this is a new skill for you, use these steps to guide you during the conversation and know that eventually, this technique will become more intuitive. In this example, you are the listener.

Step 1: Start the conversation with an open-ended question.

An open-ended question, sometimes called a door opener, is used to elicit more than a one-word answer from the other person. It "opens the door" to a good dialogue.

You: I want to save more money for the kids' college education. What do you think?

Partner: I don't know. I do worry that if we don't save more now we won't have enough to send them to the college of their choice in the future. But I also want to enjoy our lives as a family now.

Step 2: Ask clarifying questions to learn more.

A clarifying question helps you get more data about the other person's perspective to increase mutual understanding, but does so without attempting to problem-solve or offer your opinion.

You: How is saving more for the kids' education connected to enjoying our lives now?

Partner: Well, if we put more money in their education fund, then we have less to spend on the fun things we do as a family now. It costs a lot to ski and travel with them. I don't think we can afford to do both.

Step 3: Reflect back what you heard to ensure accuracy.

When reflecting back to your partner, try to use their exact words whenever possible.

You: What I hear you saying is if we save more for the kids' education now, then we will have less to spend on fun family activities now. You don't think we can afford to do both. Did I hear you correctly?

Partner: Yes, you heard me correctly. I also think we need to make sure we are modeling good financial behavior so the kids learn how to save money, not just spend it.

Step 4: Ask more clarifying questions.

Asking clarifying questions is a great way to drill down and discover more information about your partner and learn more about their money mindset. In this example, the listener asks only two clarifying questions, but in real life you can ask many more.

You: How do you want to model good financial behavior?

Partner: Maybe we could talk with the kids about this dilemma. It might be a good way to show them that even as adults you have to make decisions about saving and spending, and they aren't always easy.

Step 5: Summarize the communication and thank the person for sharing.

Ending the exchange with a summary to show that you understand what the other person said is a great way to ensure good communication. It is also nice to thank the person for engaging in a money talk, as this promotes good will.

You: Okay. So, you want to save more for the kids' education and still have fun as a family now. You are worried that we can't afford to do all of those things together. You do want to teach the kids how to have healthy money habits and you think talking with them about this dilemma might be a way to do so. Thanks for letting me know.

Partner: You're welcome. Thanks for listening.

At first this communication tactic and the steps involved may seem awkward to you, but with practice, active listening comes more naturally.

Kingsbury Rule #4: Don't Mind-Read

While it may be tempting, don't try to read your partner's thoughts. Instead, ask open-ended questions to learn more about his or her money mindset. Because when you make assumptions, they are often based on *your* money mindset, not your partner's mindset in the moment. Besides, mind-reading tends to make people angry, because the person doesn't feel heard. Do yourself and your partner a favor and don't read minds.

Mind-reading is a trap that many long-term couples fall into. While time together can strengthen the relationship, it also gives you a lot of data on how your partner has reacted to financial issues in the past. The tendency is to assume that your partner's actions and motives are still the same as they were in the past. Every conversation and situation is different, so it's vital to not jump to conclusions.

Using active listening when you talk about money is a great way to avoid this trap. It allows you to find out more about your partner's spending, saving, gifting, or investing behavior and makes it almost impossible to mind-read.

Kingsbury Rule #5: Practice Curiosity

Bring a healthy dose of curiosity to every money conversation. To do this, pretend you are a scientist interviewing a subject for a research project. Ask thoughtful, clarifying question to learn more about your partner's perspective on the financial matter at hand. When you are busy wondering about where the other person is coming from, you learn more and your mind is too preoccupied to pick a fight!

Curiosity is a great tool for increasing mutual understanding and improving communication between partners. Because curiosity plays such an important part in having a successful financial dialogue, the next chapter is dedicated to exploring how to use curiosity, especially when the conversation is difficult or highly charged.

Kingsbury Rule #6: Agree to Disagree

Tread lightly and agree to disagree before you engage in a money dialogue. The goal is to understand each other's viewpoint, to keep an open mind, and to lay the groundwork for more financial dialogues in the future. It is *not* to win the argument. From time to time, you and your loved one won't agree and no matter how much you discuss it, you will each view the situation differently. Instead of getting caught up by the fact that you don't agree, embrace it. Differences make life interesting and rich.

As Marla learned, being more mature could really help when it comes to financial conversations. She is now in her sixties and has been remarried for over 10 years. In her first marriage, Marla learned that fighting about money and always having to be right was not the best approach to resolving conflict. In her second marriage, she took a different approach. "I realized that you don't always see things the same way as your partner; you respond differently. You react at a different speed. It was an 'aha' moment for me."[3]

Even when you agree to disagree, the money talk should still be considered successful. The goal is mutual understanding, not total agreement. If you learned something new about the other person, then it was a worthwhile conversation.

Kingsbury Rule #7: Give Yourself a Reward

Reward yourself and your partner after each financial conversation. Together, you have taken a proactive step toward financial health and wellness and you deserve some recognition. The reward doesn't need to be expensive or extravagant. It can be as simple as taking a walk around your neighborhood, watching your favorite show on Netflix, or giving each other a high five. Coupling a positive experience with every financial conversation reinforces that money talk is an enjoyable experience.

Brian and I use the reward system whenever we have a financial conversation. Because we like the outdoors, we typically treat ourselves to a hike or long bike ride after a money talk. If the conversation was tense, the exercise helps us release any frustration. We both love nature and doing an activity outdoors always makes us feel more connected to each other. There is nothing like climbing a mountain to put your life and financial concerns back in perspective.

Despite the pressure to remain silent about your finances, engaging in money conversations and learning to fight fair financially are important skills. You were not born knowing how to identify, discuss, and resolve money conflicts. But you can master this skill now. It is worth the investment of time and energy, because discussing financial matters with ease and grace certainly makes managing money as a couple a lot more fun.

It Takes Two to Tango

Talking openly and honestly about money takes two people. You may really want to find out more about your partner's elderly mother's financial situation, but he won't open up about it. Or you may want to develop a household budget but your spouse keeps making excuses as to why today is not a good time to start the conversation. It is not unusual for one person to want to discuss finances more than the other. Any revolution starts with a brave soul like you wanting to change the status quo. But what do you do when you want to discuss money matters with a loved one and they are just not interested?

You need to feel your feelings. You may feel disappointed, sad, hurt, angry, or frustrated. You may even feel relieved, especially if you were anxious or uncomfortable anticipating how this money talk would unfold. No matter what emotions you experience, validate them and give yourself time to feel them. Change takes time, especially when it comes to shifting family dynamics and communication patterns. In some situations, it takes a lot of time! Be patient and know that it is not unusual to run into roadblocks before you are able to break through money silence in your partnership or family.

While there is no magic wand that you can wave and make your partner agree to talk about money, there are useful communication tactics to employ. So if you find that you are the only one wanting to dance, try one (or all) of the following three techniques.

The Broken Record Technique

This technique is named after the sound of a skipping vinyl record on an old-time record player. If there's a scratch on the record, the needle keeps replaying the same few bars of music—over and over again. When it comes to asking another person to talk about money, it may take several tries. You may need to request this conversation over and over again, like a broken record. It is important not to hound the person by making too many requests in a short period of time (which can feel like nagging). For example, asking to discuss money matters several times a day is too much. But gently requesting a financial conversation every so often may help the other person realize that this request is important to you and your desire to talk about money will not go away. Eventually the other party might surprise you and say, "Okay, let's talk."

The Teachable Moment Strategy

This is a great technique for talking to children about money, but it works with partners too! A teachable moment is a spontaneous event that triggers an opportunity to discuss money with another person. For example, suppose you are holiday shopping with your girlfriend and she throws a pair of new jeans for herself in your cart. Instead of judging her for this action, stop and get curious about her decision. Gently ask her about the jeans and what is motivating her to buy them now, when you were supposed to be holiday shopping for other people. Being curious and asking an open-ended question decreases the likelihood of your girlfriend getting defensive. Then let the conversation unfold. Chances are this type of teachable moment will educate both of you about your shared values, and how you make financial decisions.

The Critical Moment Method

Beginning a financial conversation during a family emergency is not an ideal situation. However, critical moments are often the time when a resistant partner is willing to open up about money matters. A crisis, such as a health scare, the loss of a loved one, or a pending divorce, often triggers the need for a money talk. For example, if your partner has a heart attack, he may be open to discussing your estate plan with the children if the crisis made him appreciate how precarious life can be. Or your favorite aunt dies without a will and family chaos ensues. Your wife now understands why talking with your advisor about legacy planning makes sense.

Critical moments force all of us to put our lives in perspective. We sober up and realize our lives are finite. This is the end of magical thinking, according to Kathleen Rehl, PhD, CFP®, CeFT®, and author of *Moving Forward on Your Own: A Financial Guidebook for Widows*. Rehl explains that if you say, "If I die someday . . ." then you are living in a dream world. "The misconception is that if we don't think about death then it won't happen." Her response is direct. "That's the divine plan. We are *all* going to die someday." Rehl believes that when the spell of magical thinking is broken, there is an opportunity to talk about finances in a realistic way.[4]

A caution: tread lightly with this tactic. Critical moments require you to be sensitive to the situation and careful with your timing. However, if your partner appears to be more emotionally available to discuss the financial aspects of the crisis, then it may be time to have a money talk. Remember to keep the conversation brief. If emotions run too high, as they can during a crisis, know that you can revisit the dialogue when life settles back down a bit.

Starting a money talk with a partner who is not sold on the idea of breaking money silence is a worthwhile endeavor, but challenging. If the process seems slow and laborious, or you simply want support, working with a coach, counselor, or a trusted advisor can be a good idea. A professional skilled in financial psychology and communication acts as a neutral sounding board and can help you brainstorm next steps based on your unique situation.

In my experience, family dynamics usually shift slowly and change begins after one family member makes a commitment to examine their relationship with money. Other loved ones tend to jump on board later after they witness the positive impact on this brave person's financial and personal life.

Progress, Not Perfection

Talking about money as a couple is not a one-time event. It is a journey that requires communication skills training and practice. To think you are going to start a financial dialogue and be a master communicator out of the gate is unrealistic. As with any skill, you need to practice, practice, and then practice some more. And when you finish practicing, you still won't be perfect. But you will be better! The goal is progress, not perfection.

Learning how to break money silence and talk to your partner about finances requires the same stamina as training for a sporting event. Take Serena Williams, one of the greatest professional tennis players of all time, for example. She is ranked No. 1 by the Women's Tennis Association, has won 36 total grand slam tournaments and four Olympic gold medals, and many more accolades.[5] But she wasn't born knowing how to play tennis. She had to learn the game's basic skills, and then practiced for hours, days, and years until she was proficient enough to compete on the world stage. Any athlete or expert will tell you that mastery of a skill requires repetition, a willingness to make and learn from mistakes, and a tenacity to hang in there when things get tough.

The good news: learning how to talk with your partner about money is not as labor-intensive as training to be a professional athlete. But it does require a commitment of time and energy to be successful. You need to make it a priority as a couple. Otherwise the inertia of money silence may keep you stuck right where you are.

Below are a few ideas on how you can begin to practice your money talk skills. Try these suggestions and feel free to come up with your own ideas. These discussions don't have to be boring. They actually can be entertaining and fun. So be creative and think outside of the box when it comes to exploring your relationship with money together.

Go on a Money Vacation[6]

Imagine that you are a tourist visiting an island where only your partner knows the financial language. This language is based on his money scripts, mindset, and history. You are visiting this money island for the first time and need to learn more about the island culture, customs, and money scripts that influence the native islanders' financial habits. As with any visit to a foreign country, your objective is not to change the culture or to teach the residents how to adopt your money practices but to learn as much as you can about the culture during your stay.

Begin this conversation with your partner giving you a quick tour of his money island. This tour includes some of the island's key money scripts, traditions, and decision-making practices. Your goal as a vacationer is to ask your tour guide open-ended questions to learn as much as you can about this exotic place. You don't share your thoughts or opinions, as you know that your partner will also get a chance to visit *your* money island soon.

The first time you go on a money vacation, keep the trip short, about 10 to 15 minutes. This way your partner will also have time to visit your money island and play the tourist. Once you are done with this activity and you both have gone on a money vacation, share your experiences with each other. Talk about what you admired about the foreign land and indicate what things you found interesting about this place. You may even want to borrow one or two money scripts for a week to see how they work on your island.

If you continue these excursions through several money discussions, you eventually will discover a new money island. In creating this new place, focus on picking customs and money scripts from your partner's island and having your partner do the same. That place, called "Our Money Island," will then be made up of the best of both worlds.

Listen to the "Breaking Money Silence" Podcast

In 2016, I started a podcast series called "Breaking Money Silence." In each episode, I interview a guest about a money myth that they want to bust open so they can have a healthier relationship with money. The myths explored include "You have to work so hard for money," "Family finances should be managed and controlled by one person," and "You are a prisoner of your money history." I tape new episodes monthly so there are many more myths to explore. Each podcast is only 20 minutes long and available free on iTunes or Google Play. Or visit http://www.break-ingmoneysilence.com/podcast for the latest episodes.

I encourage you to listen the "Breaking Money Silence" podcasts together. Then discuss the myth addressed in that episode and let the conversation unfold. This is an entertaining and quick way to build in a money talk each week.

Share Your Money Talk Challenge Answers

The end of each chapter in this book features Money Talk Challenges. Each of these activities is designed to provide you with insight into your relationship with money and your ability to talk about finances. Use these activities as a tool for starting a money discussion with your partner. Complete the exercises separately, then spend 15 minutes sharing your responses and what you learned from the activity. In the beginning, keep these dialogues short, knowing you can always revisit a Money Talk Challenge and discuss it further at a later date.

Summary

In this chapter, you learned about money compatibility and ways to be brave about breaking money silence. Remember these key points.

- Money compatibility is an important factor to consider in a romantic relationship.

- Myths about conflict present a roadblock for couples that want to talk about money.

- Fighting about finances happens in a healthy relationship and can increase intimacy, as long as you learn to fight fair financially.

- The "Kingsbury Rules of Fighting Fair Financially" offer guidelines for better handling of money conflicts.

- There are several tactics for beginning a money talk in a fun and creative way, especially if your partner is reluctant to break money silence with you.

Money Talk Challenge: Building Your Active Listening Muscles

The only way to build your active listening muscles is through practice and repetition. This activity is designed to help you do just that. You will need a study partner. This person can be a loved one, an advisor, a coach, or trusted friend. A word of caution: If you and your loved one fight about money, or have a lot of tension around finances, select a different study partner. In time, you can do this activity with the person you tend to fight with, but first you need to become more comfortable with listening in this manner.

Instructions

Set aside 20 minutes to fully complete this challenge. You and your study partner will each get five minutes to be the listener. When you are not the listener, then you will be the speaker. Once both of you have had a chance to play both roles, you will spend 10 minutes discussing the experience using the following questions. Toss a coin to decide who will be the first listener.

Step 1: The first listener starts by asking her partner, "What are you most proud of financially?" The listener's goal is to actively listen to the answer and follow the active listening formula to gain a clear understanding of the speaker's communication. Keep the dialogue going until the five minutes is up. It helps to set a timer so you can focus on the conversation instead of time keeping. At first this may feel like a long time, but eventually when you become more proficient in listening, the time will pass more quickly.

Step 2: Once you are done with this first conversation, take one or two minutes to answer the following questions in writing.

Listener's Questions:

1. What was it like to actively listen to your partner?

2. What insights did you gain about this person that you might have missed otherwise?

3. What did you learn about yourself while you were listening?

Speaker's Questions:

1. Using a scale of "1" (lowest) to "5" (highest), how well did the listener actively listen?

2. Name one skill the listener excelled at during the conversation.

3. Name one area for improvement and an idea about how to work on this skill.

Step 3: Do not share your answers now. Instead, switch roles and repeat the exercise.

Step 4: Once you have both role-played each part, take the remaining time to share your answers and discuss your experience as both the listener and the speaker.

Step 5: After this debriefing session, complete the following statements as a way of improving your listening skills:

1. The action I will take to improve my listening skills is . . .

2. I will complete this action step by . . .

3. My accountability partner for this action step is . . .

For Advisors

Complete the activity above to practice your active listening skills. Even if you are skilled in this area, a little more practice never hurts. Next, ask a colleague or trusted staff member to sit in on a client meeting with you. Have them observe your active listening skills. After the meeting has ended, and the clients have departed, sit down with your observer and have them share their impressions of your listening skills. Use the following prompts as a guide for feedback and discussion.

1. Your strongest listening skill is: (circle your response)

    Asking open-ended questions

Asking clarifying questions

Reflecting back what is heard

Showing empathy for the client's concerns

Mirroring the body language of the client

Other: (list a specific skill)

2.   An example of how you used this skill in the meeting is . . .

3.   One area you could strengthen is: (circle your response)

Asking open-ended questions

Asking clarifying questions

Reflecting back what is heard

Showing empathy for the client's concerns

Mirroring the body language of the client

Other: (list a specific skill)

4.   An example of how you could have used this skill in the meeting is . . .

Complete this exercise every quarter to continue to improve your active listening skills.

CHAPTER SIX

Curiosity Killed the Cat but Saved the Conversation

The important thing is not to stop questioning. Curiosity has its own reason for existing.

—Albert Einstein

Avery is a rambunctious six-year-old feline that Brian and I rescued from a shelter. She is full of personality and very entertaining. Avery has a quest for knowledge and is always exploring the nooks and crannies of our house. Even though she has been with us for three years, she remains fiercely curious about her surroundings. I find her in the strangest places. One day she is on top of the washer-dryer in the laundry room. The next day she is sleeping in a canvas bag in my closet. Her newest trick is hiding underneath the living room coffee table flat as a pancake. She stays there until I have looked everywhere for her, then she pops out and meows at me. It's almost as she is saying, "Gotcha!"

Avery is a cat that could just settle for basking in the sun on the back of the living room couch. Instead, she is on a never-ending quest for adventure. In Avery's world, there is always something new to learn and discover. I guess this is where the saying, "Curiosity killed the cat" comes from. But in Avery's case, curiosity is what keeps her life fun and interesting. I think you and I could learn a thing or two from Avery. Curiosity not only makes your life richer but also makes conversations better.

When it comes to financial conversations, especially difficult ones, wondering about the other person's money mindset and decision-making process is a vital skill. A healthy dose of curiosity helps you step outside your own mindset so you can explore someone else's financial attitudes. It aids in mutual understanding and decreases the likelihood of getting in a fight. Yes, curiosity can turn a difficult talk into one that is meaningful and gratifying.

As adults, we can lose our natural instincts to be curious. We are busy going to work, raising a family, and paying the bills. Who has time to wonder about the world around you? I know I didn't. The funny thing is I didn't realize that my own curiosity was woefully underdeveloped until I attended a coaching course on the topic. I enrolled, as it was a required class for my certification, not because I was inquisitive about the subject matter. That fact alone should have given me a clue!

The first day of the course, the professor introduced the topic of curiosity as a listening skill. That night she gave us a homework assignment designed to help us practice our curiosity. The assignment was to lie on your back and look up under the kitchen sink for 30 minutes. After the time expired, you had to write about your experience.

My first thought after hearing the assignment was "I can't believe I am paying good money to take this course." I went home that night truly believing that the teacher had lost her mind. I decided that the assignment was a waste of my time and didn't complete it. As a type A student, not doing my homework was a big deal. But I felt strongly that I could learn more from reading a book for 30 minutes than lying under my sink.

The next day, my fellow students discussed the assignment and shared their experiences. As I listened to the classroom discussion, I quickly realized you could learn a lot from lying under your sink with a curious mind. These individuals learned about pipes and plumbing, and also discovered important things about themselves. The students who completed the homework learned to ask questions about what they saw, to not jump to conclusions about how their mind wandered, and to use their natural sense of curiosity to acquire new information about the world around them.

I learned that I was not that curious. For years, I had made assumptions based on my life experiences. I had jumped to conclusions too quickly and not wondered enough about other people's thoughts, feelings, and motives. While this realization was a bit painful, it was a big aha moment for me. It seemed that I needed to be more like my cat Avery.

The good news is listening with a healthy dose of curiosity is a skill that you can relearn. I know because practice has made me much more proficient at asking open-ended questions and letting go of assumptions.

My friends tease me, as I apparently say, "What is that about for you?" in almost every one of my conversations. The funny thing is, I really want to know.

Whether you are in touch with your natural curiosity or need to reconnect with it, this skill is vital when breaking money silence in your life. So whether you are talking about money with your partner, your parents, or your children, curiosity makes the conversation better.

Tapping into Your Beginner's Mind

According to the Merriam-Webster dictionary, the definition of *curiosity* is "a desire to know, an inquisitive interest to know; or interest leading to inquiry." When you are truly curious, your head is filled with questions and each answer sparks a new inquiry, and you're in a place where you just can't get enough information. Young children have a natural curiosity and constantly wonder out loud about what they see around them. Questions such as "But why, Mommy?" and "What is that, Daddy?" are commonplace. Unfortunately, if this type of questioning is not encouraged, it wanes with age.

In Zen Buddhism, there is a principle called "beginner's mind." This is an attitude of openness that requires you to let go of preconceived notions when studying a subject or interacting with another person. To help you reconnect with your childlike wonder and curiosity, use beginner's mind as you explore your money mindset and break money silence with others. This practice involves approaching every conversation as if it was your first. It requires that you stay open to all possibilities and let go of any judgments based on previous life experiences. Since it is impossible to let go of all your preconceived notions, the goal is to notice these thoughts and let them float by as opposed to verbalizing or reacting to them.

While curiosity doesn't cure all money problems, it does alleviate many of the things that cause a money talk to go off track. It will temper your need to be right, to prove your point, or to convince the other party that they are wrong. Using your beginner's mind will help you learn more about yourself and the other person. In other words, it will increase mutual understanding. And as you learned earlier, that is the goal of any good financial conversation.

Tapping into beginner's mind can be challenging for some people. This is especially true if you work in a profession like financial planning, engineering, or technology, where you are trained and paid to solve problems. It also can be counterintuitive if you are hardwired to fix a situation not discuss your thoughts and feelings about it. But we were all kids once, so we all have the capacity to use our beginner's mind. It just may take some time and practice to plug back into this mindset of wonder and curiosity.

Don't worry. I am not going to ask you to lie underneath your kitchen sink so you can learn more about curiosity. But I am going to suggest that you notice your tendencies to jump to conclusions or make quick decisions without tapping into your beginner's mind and examining all the possibilities. Doing so is a sign that you may need to become more inquisitive in your financial life. Here are some other signs that indicate it may be time for you to build up your curiosity muscle:

- You finish other people's sentences.
- You know there is a right way or a wrong way to do things.
- You don't have time to hear the other person's side of the story.
- You have seen this situation a thousand times.
- Your loved one always acts this way.

If any of these statements resonate with you, it may be time to reconnect with your beginner's mind. Trust me. As one previously not-so-curious person to another, the benefits of being less judgmental and being more inquisitive are well worth the effort. Not only will you have more productive money conversations, you will discover new things about yourself and others. You will build trust with other people and you will demonstrate that you care about their experience in the world. If you work as an advisor, curiosity is the key to connecting with your clients so you can best serve their needs. If you are a partner, parent, sibling, or child, wondering out loud is a great way to strengthen your relationships and model for the next generation the value of staying curious your entire life.

Goodbye Judgment, Hello Curiosity

Be honest with yourself. Have you ever judged another person for his or her financial decisions or habits? Maybe you didn't say anything out loud, but you passed judgment in your head. You may have thought "I would never waste that much money on dinner." Or "I can't believe she spent that much on a new purse." Chances are you have criticized someone, at least one time in your life, for a financial behavior that didn't fit with your money mindset.

Why are we so judgmental when it comes to finances? For one thing, we have been taught that there is a right way and a wrong way to manage money and that finance is a purely rational activity. However, as I have discussed in previous chapters of this book, money is emotional and people make financial decisions based on their feelings, values, and money mindsets. As an outsider looking in, you can't always know all the factors that went into someone else's decision-making process. But instead of getting curious and asking questions to learn more about another person's money habits, many of us remain silent in judgment.

Another factor that fuels judgment is the desire to "keep up with the Joneses." If you suffer from this syndrome, you are not alone. Many of us constantly compare ourselves to neighbors and colleagues whom we perceive to be better off, and our society is obsessed with celebrities and their wealthy lifestyles. "Reality" television shows fill the airwaves with images of people who live in the lap of luxury. The success of these shows depends on viewers simultaneously wanting what these celebrities have and judging them for having it. Watching programs like these probably makes you feel good and bad about yourself all at the same time. The underlying message is that somehow you are doing it "wrong" when it comes to money if you can't have what they have.

But trying to keep up with the proverbial Joneses fuels money shame and silence. It puts your focus in the wrong place. You set your sights on the external world as opposed to your internal experience. But if you get curious and look within, you can learn so much about yourself and develop more empathy for those around you.

What would it be like if you watched one of these programs with a beginner's mind? Imagine watching and wondering about a Kardashian's money mindset instead of criticizing her for the dress she is wearing or the husband she currently has. Boy, that would be different, wouldn't it?

You could do the same thing in real life. The next time you find out your adult brother bought a second motorcycle while still living with your parents, why not ask him how he made that decision? No accusatory tone. No judgment. Just curiosity. You may be surprised by his answer. Maybe he is staying with your parents because he is worried about them, not because he is a freeloader. You never know until you ask.

The financial services industry also contributes to our collective lack of curiosity. While every advisor is different, the field is comprised largely of people who take a purely mathematical approach to investments and financial planning. (If you are an advisor reading this book, you are probably an exception to this rule.) I'm willing to bet that if you work with (or are) a professional who is certified as a financial planner or analyst, that person's training did not include skills training on communicating about money and how to be curious about financial behaviors. Instead, the coursework required for advisors is concentrated almost exclusively on the technical aspects of finance and investing. Thus, when you visit an advisor, you most likely get the message, either by design or unintentionally, that managing money is a cut-and-dried, emotionless endeavor. This reinforces the all-or-nothing, judgmental approach to finance.

There is a long history of money being viewed through the lens of rigid rules and rational thinking. But it is time to add a healthy dose of curiosity to the mix. By doing so, you will gain valuable insight into your own money mindset and decision-making process. You also will find out more about how the people in your life think and act around money. This exploration is likely to soften your heart, help you appreciate differences, and foster productive and meaningful financial conversations.

Get Curious about Retirement

Did you know that almost half of couples disagree on their exact retirement age and one in three couples is not on the same page when it comes to their expected lifestyle when they retire?[1] Often, couples don't figure out that they have diverse views until they sit down with an advisor to discuss planning for this next phase of life.

This is exactly what happened to my friends, Dan and Karen. At their first advisory meeting Karen explained to the advisor that she wanted to travel across country in an RV once the couple retired. Dan was shocked, "My ideal retirement would be getting a part-time job that had little to no stress. I would do something fun as opposed to something I had to do to make money," It was a big aha moment for the couple. Like many partners, they assumed they were on the same page with how they wanted to age together and then discovered they needed to devote some time to sharing their visions.

Discussing your retirement vision with your partner is a great place to practice curiosity. It can be fun to dream about how you will spend your golden years together, and it also is vital to planning for a secure financial future. If you work with an advisor, discuss the matter at a joint meeting. If you don't have an advisor, consider using the following questions to begin the dialogue. (If you are not in a relationship, you can still use these inquiries as a guide for engaging in this money talk with a friend, a sibling, or a coach about your retirement dreams.)

1. What would an ideal day in retirement look like for you?
2. Where would you live, and whom would you live with or by?

3. How much time would you like to spend together versus apart?
4. What values do you want to honor in this next phase of your life and what activities will you engage in that will express these values?
5. What are you most excited and most fearful about when it comes to retirement?

The goal of this conversation is to practice curious listening. Ask open-ended questions and be open to learning more about yourself and your partner. Suspend any preconceived notions or judgments. There will be time going forward to work out the specifics; for now, remain open to all the possibilities. This will help you tap into your beginner's mind and see how far curiosity can take you.

Roadblocks to Curiosity

There are a few barriers that can get in the way of having a curious money conversation. These include the desire to always be the expert, insisting on getting your way, or believing that the other person knows what is best for you. Let's look at each one of these roadblocks and how you can overcome them.

Expert Mentality

Being an expert is nice, but it can get in the way of having an honest dialogue about money. Experts tell people what to do and what to think. Advisors give recommendations. Bankers tell you how to get approved for a loan. Parents tell you to eat your vegetables with dinner. Siblings give you their opinion. You get the idea. But in a money conversation, you must take off your expert hat and replace it with your curiosity cap. If you don't, then there is a power differential that will mostly likely block a collaborative dialogue.

Instead of being an expert, take on the role of a supportive coach. A good coach, whether a sports coach or an executive coach, asks open-ended questions, actively listens, and cheers the other person on. There is a spirit of collaboration. This is distinctly different than acting as an expert.

I realize this coach-like stance may be easier for some of you to take than it will be for others. For example, if you are an advisor, your clients sometimes ask for recommendations based on your knowledge and expertise. This means that shifting from an interpersonal style of knowing to one of wondering may prove challenging. But as with any new habit, practice makes it easier. Besides, it will help you build your business, as the most successful advisors are the ones with the best listening skills.

Lou Tranquilli, the financial advisor mentioned in Chapter 1, is a great example of a professional who adopted a coach-like mentality and increased his revenue as a result. A few years ago, Lou decided to form a women's advisory group to help him understand the best way to meet the needs of his female clients. He asked the group curious, open-ended questions and really listened to their answers. Lou let go of being an expert and embraced the role of a collaborator and coach. In the first year, his business revenues increased by 25 percent. And all it took was letting go of being right and getting curious instead.[2]

The "You Know Better" Mentality

The "you know better" mentality is the opposite of being an expert. This mindset happens when you relinquish control and let other people make decisions for you. Often this mentality is born out of fear. You may worry about making a bad financial or investment decision. Or you may fear that you are not as knowledgeable as your partner, parent, sibling, or advisor, and you defer to the other party.

Sharon is a good example of a person with the "you know better" mentality. She is college-educated, the mother of two children, and the wife of a scientist. Despite being intelligent and more than capable of learning more about finance, Sharon defers all investment decisions to her husband. The problem is that her husband is a talented scientist but not a great investor and could use his wife's input. But Sharon likes the idea of not having to think about money and just focus on raising the children.

For Sharon, as well as others like her, there is a short-term advantage to this mentality. You get to remain childlike in your approach to money. If you have a partner or loved one who makes all your financial decisions, then you never have to take responsibility for this part of your life. But there is a very big downside. The disadvantage is that you lose out on the opportunity to become more self-aware and empowered. You also miss out on a chance to connect with and learn more about your partner. Believe it or not, being knowledgeable about the family finances boosts your self-confidence and it increases intimacy in your relationships.

In my experience, more women than men suffer from this mentality. Women from the traditional and baby boomer generations were socialized to believe that men are more equipped to make financial decisions. While this is not true, and there is no research that indicates that men are financially more astute than women, the myth lives on. Unfortunately, this mentality puts some women at high risk. The story of a widow who had relied solely on her husband to handle the financial planning and is suddenly forced into a new role at the same time she is grieving the loss of her spouse is all too common.

Kelly Shikany, CFP®, of Lakeside Wealth Management, shared one of these sad stories with me. One of her clients is an 84-year-old widow who had depended on her husband to manage all the financial matters their entire married life. After he died, Kelly met with the woman and explained that all the accounts in her deceased husband's name needed to be changed to her name. The client became overwhelmed by this simple task, and remains to this day fearful that she will run out of money to live on. While Kelly assures her that she is financially secure, the client doesn't believe her and irrationally worries about running out of money. Her fear sometimes turns into anger at her three adult children, who have grown to resent her. They want her to hire professional home health services but she refuses.

Here's Kelly's perspective, "I really love working with this woman as she is great lady and she truly loves her children. She is just scared. I really wish she had been involved in the family finances throughout her life—she would be more familiar with the planning process, and not be so fearful now to spend money on the care that she desperately needs."[3]

Most advisors have a heart-breaking story or two like this one, and even one is too many.

My Way Mentality

As singer Frank Sinatra crooned in his famous 1969 anthem of independence and empowerment, "I did it my way." However, when you are talking about money, always doing it your way is problematic. It doesn't allow for an open dialogue with the other person and it is a barrier to curiosity. Yes, your partner can wonder about why you do what you do financially, but if you take a "my way or the highway" approach, then you fail to wonder and learn about his or her experience. It is a missed opportunity to connect and grow together.

It is not unusual for a couple to have one partner with a "my way" mentality and the other with a "you know better" mentality. While these two attitudes can work together, the partners' lack of curiosity may block them from truly knowing each other and their respective money mindsets and history. While this dynamic is more common in couples in their late 60s, 70s, and 80s, it can occur in partnerships between younger people.

This dynamic worked for Walter and Toni most of their lives. Walter, the primary breadwinner of the family, made all the financial and investment decisions and very much lived with a "my way mentality." Toni worked part-time most of their marriage, and was fine deferring to Walter when it came to money matters. She enjoyed not having to "waste time meeting with their advisor" and relished her "you know better" mindset. However, when Walter announced he planned to retire in a year and move to Florida so he could play golf daily, Toni refused to follow him. She wanted to stay in their current home where she was an active member of the local community. Walter was shocked that Toni didn't agree with his plan; she had never disagreed with one of his financial decisions. Instead of getting curious as to why, he became more entrenched in his "my way mentality." Eventually, Walter moved to Florida and Toni stayed in their original home most of the year. Unfortunately, this couple did not know how to engage in a healthy money conversation and collaborate on finding solutions that worked for both of them. So they lived apart most of the year.

If you identify with this dynamic, I challenge you to switch places with your partner for one conversation. See what it feels like to make all the decisions, or experience what comes with relinquishing control. At the end of this experiment you may decide to meet in the middle, or keep things status quo. Either way, you have at least wondered what your partner's role in your financial relationship feels like and you have opened the door to wondering why you prefer your role as it currently stands.

It is impossible to be curious and open-minded all the time. Therefore, you may see yourself in one or more of these mindsets. Don't fret. There is a time and place for everything. There are times when you need to be an expert, or you need to exert or relinquish control. But when talking about money with a loved one, it is best to leave these personas behind. In the short run, it may make you feel a little vulnerable. But in the long run, it increases your chances of having an open and honest dialogue.

Now that you know the value of curiosity and the roadblocks to look out for, it's time to learn how being inquisitive can make a difficult money conversation more productive.

The Role of Curiosity in Difficult Conversations

For 15 years, I worked as a counselor specializing in eating disorders and body image issues. Eating disorders such as anorexia and bulimia have the highest mortality rate of any psychiatric illness. Part of my role was hospitalizing a person who had symptoms that placed her mental or physical health in danger. As you can imagine, I had my fair share of young women angry with me. As someone who came from a conflict-avoidant family, I found this extremely challenging until I discovered the role of curiosity in a difficult conversation. Suddenly I was not defending my decision to hospitalize the person, I was wondering about her reaction to my decision. And the more I got curious about her feelings, the less defensive she became. Curiosity actually brought us closer together at a time where the relationship could have been broken beyond repair.

I realize that talking about money is a very different situation than discussing eating disorders. But taking a curious stance in a difficult conversation is a transferable skill. Anytime someone has uncomfortable or strong emotions about money, it helps to get curious (whether it's about yourself or the other person). Wondering about the other person's thoughts and feelings decreases your defensiveness. It increases your ability to be empathetic and to actively listen. Ultimately, it allows you to engage in a productive financial conversation. Instead of fighting about finances, you find mutual understanding.

George and Carrie are a good example of how being more curious in your approach to your partner makes a difficult conversation more productive. When I first met this couple, they were hardly speaking to each other. George had contacted me to discuss his wife's spending problem. As they sat on the couch in my office, the tension between them was palpable. George felt that Carrie's shopping was out of control and vowed that if she didn't stop spending money, he would divorce her. Carrie was equally frustrated and felt that George was cheap and that his perception that her spending was out of control was absurd. "He darns his socks before he will buy a new pair. That is how cheap he is," she fumed. Clearly, they were at an impasse.

During our appointment, I asked curious, open-ended questions of each of them to uncover their different perspectives. It turned out that George really didn't like to spend money and came from an affluent family who penny-pinched for fear of losing their fortune. Carrie was raised in a lower-middle-class family where money was always tight. She described growing up and wearing hand-me-down clothes. Now that she was an adult, she enjoyed the freedom and capacity to buy brand-new designer clothes. The more money she spent, the angrier George got. And the angrier George got, the more she spent. It was a vicious cycle.

Over the course of a few meetings, I educated George and Carrie about money mindsets and taught them how to actively listen to each other. While they made some progress, George and Carrie remained convinced that the other person's money habits were wrong. George maintained his expert mentality, stating that he had studied finance in college and thus knew more than Carrie when it came to money matters. Carrie held firm in her "my way" approach. She was not going to return to feeling deprived as she did in her childhood.

One day I decided to tell them they were both right. George was correct in his desire to save, and Carrie was spot on in her desire to spend. They looked at me quizzically and asked, "How can we both be right?" I explained that each of them was an expert on their own experience in the world. However, what they needed to do to work through this conflict in their relationship was to get very curious about their partner's money mindset and how their thoughts fueled their financial habits. I asked each of them to act like a scientist and gather data about each other, and suspend judgment until the end of the session.

They took my advice, and *really* listened to each other for the first time. George discovered that Carrie felt a lot of shame as a young girl when she was forced to wear her sister's old clothes. She really feared that if she was put on a budget and could not shop as she pleased, she would feel awful and fall into a depression. Carrie learned that George was very afraid of losing his family's money. From a young age he was told stories about relatives who wasted their wealth and ended up estranged from the family. He explained that when he was younger he saved all his money and spent very little in order to win his parents' approval. Now as an adult, he didn't know how to do anything differently.

At the end of the appointment, I asked each of them to tell me what this curious conversation was like for each of them. Both expressed a newfound empathy for their partner. While there was more work ahead of them, George and Carrie had made an important discovery. Being curious during a money conversation yielded better results than remaining stubbornly focused on being right.

Breaking money silence is well worth the effort. For George and Carrie, countless other couples, and families, talking about money brought them closer together. Now that you see the benefits of sharing your thoughts and feelings about money, let's look at how you can set the stage for having a successful money talk each time.

Best Practices for Engaging in Money Talks

Dramatic screenplays and books often follow a three-act structure. They have a beginning, a middle, and an end. The same is true for a money conversation. Act one is the preparation, where you determine your goals and objectives for the conversation. Act two is the actual meeting with the person or family members. Act three is the follow-up after the meeting, where you take the action steps agreed upon in act two. When you anticipate a financial conversation may be emotionally difficult for you, the other person, or both of you, this structure can help set you up for success. Let's look individually at each act in the money conversation and how you can set yourself up for success during each one.

Act One: Prepare for the Money Talk

Any performer knows that good preparation is the key to success. The same philosophy applies to financial conversations, especially if you are discussing a difficult situation such as paying for home healthcare for your elderly dad or how to split up assets in a divorce. The preparation stage requires you to look inward and self-reflect. It also warrants looking outward and anticipating the possible thoughts and feelings of the other party. These questions will help you with this process.

1. Who do you want to engage in this money talk and for what purpose?
2. What, if anything, triggered your desire to have this conversation?
3. What specifically do you want to discuss with this person?
4. What would you consider a good outcome if this conversation went well?
5. What do you anticipate would be a good outcome for the other party?
6. What is the best way to invite this person to engage in a money talk?
7. When and where might you have this conversation?
8. What feelings might this conversation trigger for you? For the other person?
9. How might you handle these feelings if they arise?
10. If you put yourself in your money talk partner's shoes, what else should you consider as you prepare for this conversation?

You may not have all the answers to the questions above, but pondering them before your money talk is useful. At a minimum, this type of preparation triggers your curiosity and puts you in a wondering mindset.

Jamison, a 51-year-old father of two, used the questions above to prepare for an important conversation with his sister. Recently, his elderly mother had a car accident and her coworkers expressed some concerns about her memory. Jamison wanted to discuss hiring an attorney to draft some basic legal documents to protect his mother's estate should she be failing. He also wanted to find out if his sister would be willing to take their mother to the doctor to have her evaluated for memory loss. Jamison knew this would be an emotional money talk, for both himself and his sister; therefore, he took the time to prepare before calling his sister to find out when and where would be the best time for them to meet about their mother.

This type of preparation may seem cumbersome. But taking time to consider these issues in advance helps you anticipate how the dialogue could go. There are times where you won't get a chance to prepare this thoroughly and that is okay. When you *do* have some time to reflect beforehand, take advantage of it. Then use this experience when you are thrown directly into the dialogue without notice.

Act Two: The Money Talk

Act two of a money talk is the actual meeting between you and a partner, parent, child, or sibling. Eventually, you may want to invite more family members to the meeting. By doing so, you add another level of complexity based on the family and personal dynamics of the people in the room. Often it helps to have a trained mediator, such as a professional coach, family wealth consultant, or an advisor at the meeting to facilitate this process. While you are learning how to engage in a productive financial conversation, it is best to keep the dialogue between two people.

In Chapter 5, I provided guidelines for healthy money conversations. Start the meeting by reviewing these guidelines together. It helps to keep those guidelines handy and visible during the meeting. If you would like to print out a hard copy to use in your meetings, go to this link http://breakingmoneysilence.com/money-talk-guidelines and download a PDF version.

Next, set a time limit for the conversation. Keep it short, especially if you are both new to money talks, or the topic is charged. I recommend that these meetings be no longer than 30 minutes, because longer meetings make it harder to stay focused on the topic at hand. Knowing that the discussion has a definite endpoint is useful for anyone who feels anxious or uncomfortable.

During the meeting, use active listening and be curious. If you find yourself tempted to defend your position, ask an open-ended question instead. Remember your goal is to discover new information about the other person, as opposed to winning her over. Try having each money talk partner take turns, where one of you listens and the other speaks. Then halfway through the meeting, switch roles. (Refer to the Money Talk Challenge in Chapter 5 for a refresher on how to do this.) Initially, following this structure helps each of you listen and be heard. Eventually, your money conversations will become more free-flowing and organic.

If at any time the meeting gets off track or the conversation becomes heated, call a time-out. Take five minutes to get a glass of water, stretch, or simply breathe. Then pick up the conversation where you left off. Often a quick break is enough to allow you or your partner to regain focus or calm down. If it is not, then end the meeting and set a time to revisit the conversation. If you find that you don't pick up the conversation again or find it too difficult to engage in this dialogue, consider enlisting a professional counselor, coach, or advisor to act as a mediator. A neutral party in the room can be valuable when tensions are high.

At the end of the meeting, take a few minutes to collaboratively decide what action each of you will take as a result of this conversation. Determine the time frame for this follow-up activity to occur. Make sure these tasks are small and doable, as this increases the chances of success. Examples of follow-up actions include, but certainly are not limited to,

- Set a time and date for the next money talk.
- Research a particular investment, financial product, or service.
- Do a cost–benefit analysis (this is a fancy way of saying "put numbers on paper").
- Get input from another person or family member.
- Consult with your financial advisor, banker, or attorney.

Determining who will follow up and in what capacity is an important step, so don't skip it. Ending the meeting with an action plan helps both parties know that they've made progress and that this particular dialogue has ended. It also sets the stage for the next money talk.

Act Three: Follow Up and Take Action

This third act is about setting the stage for the next financial conversation. It involves taking time to reflect on the conversation, doing your homework, and then preparing for the next dialogue. Breaking money silence and talking openly and honestly about money is rarely a one-time event. It is a series of talks over weeks, months, or years.

Expect to have some feelings once the meeting has ended. You worked hard to prepare for the talk and may be relieved that it is over. You may be pleased with how receptive the other person was to discussing the matter, or a little frustrated with the outcome. Whatever you are feeling, it is okay. There is no one right way to feel after a money talk. Just don't let these feelings get in the way of following up and taking the action you promised during the discussion.

If you do get the urge to drop the ball and not discuss this matter again, or not take the action you originally agreed to, at least let your money talk partner know your intentions for doing so. This keeps the lines of communication open. But fight this urge, as money talks get better and easier over time.

Like any dramatic three-act play, money talks have moments of levity and moments of gravity. When there is humor or lightheartedness, embrace it. Laughter is a great way to connect and share an intimate moment with a family member. It is also a good release for when emotions run high. Be careful not to confuse laughing together with poking fun at someone. This type of humor should be avoided as it creates distance between you and the other party. Just know that serious money conversations don't always have to be full of doom and gloom.

Remember Jamison's story in the section on preparing for act one? He eventually talked to his sister about their mother's failing memory. The siblings agreed to meet in person for coffee at the sister's house before their mom's 75th birthday celebration. This plan allowed them to talk in person without distractions.

Overall, Jamison felt the conversation went well. As anticipated, they laughed and reminisced about their childhood, and his sister expressed frustration about being the sibling who had the greatest caregiving burden. Jamison acknowledged her feelings and thanked her for helping their mother so much. In the end, they agreed to talk to their mother about the legal paperwork and their medical concerns. Instead of doing this together, they decided to each approach her separately with the same message so as not to overwhelm her. It worked and their mother agreed to a doctor's visit and a meeting with an elder law attorney.

Jamison said that thinking about the conversation using the three-act structure was useful. "I wish it was just a three-act play with my mother. But I know that her memory is not getting better. So like it or not, there will be more financial conversations with my family in the future."

Now that you know how to break money silence in your life, there are many financial conversations you can and should have. In the next few chapters, I will share tips and tools for engaging in money talks with various members of the family. Chapter 7 addresses conversations between romantic or soon-to-be ex-romantic partners. Chapter 8 tackles the topic of talking to the next generation about money, and Chapter 9 looks at communicating with aging parents about financial matters. Select the chapters and sections of the book that speak to you and your life situation. You can always return to read a section of this book, or re-read a chapter, when and if a section becomes more pertinent to your life.

Summary

Curiosity is a wonderful ingredient to bring to the table when discussing money.

- Curiosity helps you and your loved ones learn more about each other and focus on what is important—mutual understanding.
- Being curious and open, along with practicing active listening, can make a difficult financial conversation easier and more gratifying.
- Being curious can be challenging and roadblocks such as the "expert" mentality, the "you know better" mentality, and the "my way" mentality can get in the way.
- Preparing for engaging in a potentially difficult money talk as if it is a three-act play can help you set yourself up for success.

Money Talk Challenge: Engage in a Curious Conversation Using a Money-O-Gram

A money-o-gram is like a family tree (or genogram), except instead of tracing bloodlines you're diagramming the transmission of money messages. When completed, this diagram (see Figure 6.1) contains information about how each person in your family thinks, feels, and acts around money, and how those money mindsets and patterns have been passed down from generation to generation. The money-o-gram is a great tool to use to identify, display, and discuss family patterns around finances. To complete this exercise, you will need to get curious and ask members of your family more about their relationship to money and each other.

Step 1: Start by drawing a family tree. You can use the money-o-gram diagram provided and adjust it to reflect your family, or you can draw your own. Include the two generations before you (your parents' and your grandparents' generation) and one generation after yours if you have children. If you don't have children, you can include other relatives' offspring, like nieces and nephews.

Step 2: Now fill in the details of your money-o-gram by noting each person's age, occupation, and your impression of his or her viewpoint on money and its purpose in life. If you have a blended family, make sure you include any stepparents and stepchildren as well as biological parents and children in your chart.

Step 3: Next, confirm your impressions by asking your loved ones some curious questions. Approach each of these conversations with a beginner's mind and be open to letting your preconceived impressions be replaced by what someone shares with you. If a relative is no longer living (such as a grandparent, for example), ask a living relative (son, daughter, or sibling) of that person for their impressions of this person's money personality and mindset.

The goal of this exercise is to help you engage family members in curious financial conversations. Be careful not to use the information you

Figure 6.1: Money-O-Gram

Use this diagram to fill in the names of family members. Include their ages, occupations, and a word or phrase to describe each person's money mindset. Ex. Mary, 67, chef, very frugal.

GRANDPARENTS

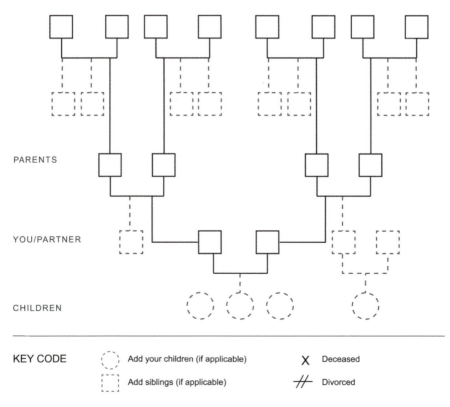

PARENTS

YOU/PARTNER

CHILDREN

KEY CODE   ⬭ Add your children (if applicable)   X   Deceased

                ⬜ Add siblings (if applicable)   ⫻   Divorced

collect to place blame on each other or other family members for past money decisions or habits. Instead, use it to foster mutual understanding.

For Advisors

Complete your own money-o-gram to see what the experience is like. Then invite a few of your clients to complete their money-o-grams with you. Remember to ask open-ended questions and listen more than you talk. The money-o-gram is a great tool to use with individual clients and couples as it helps them strengthen their money talk skills and it helps demonstrate the value of curiosity.

This coaching exercise may take longer than one meeting to complete, so once your clients comprehend how a money-o-gram works and the types of questions they should ask loved ones, ask your clients to complete the money-o-gram as homework for their next meeting with you. By doing so, you are encouraging clients to practice their money talk skills and strengthen their curiosity in between appointments. At the follow-up meeting, ask about this homework using the following questions.

1. What was it like to be curious with a family member about money?
2. What was your biggest challenge in completing this exercise?
3. What new information did you learn?
4. How might you use your money-o-gram to continue money talk with your family?
5. What did you discover about your money history that would be important for me to know?

The beauty of the money-o-gram exercise is that it teaches your clients important money talk skills and at the same time, provides you with useful information about how to best advise them. Discussing this chart with your clients provides you with a large amount of data about their family dynamics and money mindsets, in a nonthreatening way. By identifying the clients' and their families' financial and interpersonal strengths and challenges, you will be in a better position to help them plan for their financial future.

CHAPTER SEVEN

Until Death (or Divorce) Do You Part: Difficult Couple Money Conversations

All married couples should learn the art of battle as they should learn the art of making love.

—Ann Landers, syndicated advice columnist

The phone rang. It was the real estate agent telling me that our offer on the condominium was going to fall through. "Did you know about Brian's credit?" she demanded angrily. "It is horrible." I didn't know anything about his credit rating. I had never thought to ask in the two years we had been dating. The real estate agent quipped, "Why don't you just buy the house on your own? Your credit is stellar. Think about it." She hung up.

Stunned was the only way to describe what I felt in that moment. Brian and I had moved in together the year before, and recently started looking at houses to buy. I was excited that we were making a commitment to each other and I really thought this meant we would soon get engaged. Now what would happen? I didn't want to buy a condo alone. I wanted to buy my first home with the man I loved. Mr. Right, so I thought.

A very difficult money conversation followed. It turned out that Brian had no idea his credit was ruined. He had co-signed for a car loan that was unpaid by the borrower. And unbeknownst to him, his brother-in-law had stolen Brian's social security number and had taken out several other loans in Brian's name. All these loans were in default. Brian was enraged. I was livid. It was a difficult night.

We never bought that condo, and it took several years for Brian to clear up his credit. The bank that he owed money to didn't care if his sister's husband had ripped him off. They just wanted their money back, so Brian saved up and eventually paid off his brother-in-law's debt. My image of happily ever after never was the same. Money had entered the picture and reared its ugly head.

Eventually Brian proposed, we got married and bought our first home together. Brian worked diligently to clear up his credit and I am happy to say that his credit score is almost as high as mine these days. Over our 20-year marriage, we have bought and sold several houses, and had a few difficult money conversations. Remember the contractor story from Chapter 1? Let's just say I practice what I preach. Even in a good marriage, challenging financial conversations will happen. And whether you stay together until death do you part, or until you decide to split up, knowing how to engage in difficult money talk is well worth the effort.

From the time two people start dating until the time they ultimately say goodbye through death or divorce, finances are a big part of the relationship. Couples either consciously or unconsciously decide how to spend and enjoy money, how to save and amass wealth, and how to use money to exert power and control in the relationship. Some partners fight about money; others worry about it. Some couples join forces and create a strong financial and emotional bond; others never seem to trust each other financially. Whatever the dynamic in your relationship, you owe it to yourself and your partner to talk about money.

Seven out of ten romantic partners report that money causes friction in their relationship.[1] Problems range from financial squabbles to financial infidelity, defined as hiding or lying about money. Like sexual transgressions, financial infidelity erodes trust and can lead couples to separate or divorce. But money itself is not the real culprit. It is the silence around finances that festers until things eventually blow up. I can't help but think that if money talk skills were taught in schools that the divorce rate in this country would be lower.

Partners who engage in money talk once a week report being happier with their partners than couples who discuss finances every few months.[2] When asked to name the biggest money mistake they made in their relationship, couples said it was waiting too long to discuss money with their partners.[3]

In this chapter, you will learn how to engage in money conversations at various stages of a committed relationship. Many of these talks are labeled "difficult" by society. However, if you approach these conversations with personal insight, love, and mutual respect, they can be clarifying and enlightening dialogues.

The Role of Emotional Intelligence

Emotional intelligence (EI) is defined as the capacity to be aware of, control, and express one's emotions, and to handle interpersonal relationships judiciously and empathetically. Many business books discuss EI. Leaders who are emotionally savvy tend to be more successful, and employees who have high EI scores typically advance rapidly in their careers. But what about your romantic partner—does he or she need to have high EI scores? When it comes to managing money as a team, it certainly helps.

Now, I am not recommending that you give all your first dates an emotional intelligence assessment test, or that you need to leave your partner if you discover he or she has work to do in this area. But I do think it's important for you to appreciate the role emotional intelligence plays in turning a tough money talk into a productive one.

Emotional intelligence has two components. The first is being able to recognize, understand, and manage your own emotions. The second component is being able to recognize, understand, and influence the emotions of others. In a difficult money talk, good EI allows you to tap into your own feelings about the situation and appreciate your partner's feelings. It also helps you to communicate in a respectful way when tempers run high or feelings are hurt. People with high EI know when to push through a difficult conversation and when to take a time-out to calm down.

Richard and Leslie are a good example of a couple that works on having emotionally intelligent money conversations. Historically, they have approached money from vastly different money mindsets. Leslie believes that there will always be enough money, and Richard thinks there will never be enough money. As partners, they struggle when they have to make a large financial decision, and as parents, they often disagree when it comes to spending as a family. Leslie explains, "When it was just the two of us, money was never an issue. Once the kids were born, it seemed that we became adversaries when we discuss money."

Both Richard and Leslie have worked to increase their emotional intelligence. This allows them to employ techniques that help them tolerate their differences. As Leslie says, "I teach conflict management courses at the college level, and I decided to apply several conflict management tools to how we approached money discussions. Guess what? It worked!"

The couple now schedules money meetings at a time that is best for them as a couple and when their three children are not around the house. They put these meetings on the family calendar and then create a written agenda before the scheduled time. Each partner is allowed to put up to three agenda items on the list. This allows each partner to be prepared before the meeting and also helps the couple stay on track during the discussions.

A key element to their success in having productive money talks is their agreement to practice a "no blame" policy. Leslie notes, "We practice Q-TIP, known as 'quit taking it personally.' We have managed to take most of the emotions out of our money conversations. If one of us starts to get upset, we take a time-out to gather our thoughts and clear our heads. I do this more often than my husband does."

This strategy evolved over time and respects both Richard's need for structure and Leslie's need to emotionally step back when she gets over-whelmed. Leslie says, "I still don't love money conversations, and I still cringe when I see one scheduled on the calendar. However, the end result of our time together is more positive. Richard and I now act like financial partners."

If you identify with Richard and Leslie's story, you are not alone. Most couples experience times in their partnership where money is a source of conflict. What matters is how you handle these differences. Being emotionally savvy and finding ways to honor and respect each other's needs during a difficult dialogue is the key ingredient to success.

If you are interested in learning more about emotional intelligence, see the Resource Guide for recommended resources. For now, let's look at how certain stages in a relationship can trigger a difficult money talk and what you can do to best work through these challenges.

Moving from Dating to a Committed Relationship

After the flowers, candy, and expensive dinners fade away, you as a couple are left with some big decisions. Do we commit to each other? Do we move in together? Do we get married? Each of these phases in a relationship brings new financial questions to the table. When addressed proactively, these conversations bring you closer together and set you up for a good life together. But when you ignore finances, trouble may be brewing.

Eighty-eight percent of couples say that the most important reason to get married is love.[4] Only 28 percent say financial stability is just as vital. But love and money can't be separated. Once you commit to another person, especially when you get married legally, what was once yours becomes ours. While the laws vary state by state, marriage means that your spouse's income and debts are now yours as well. Often your tax rate changes, and your property and other assets may be viewed as joint. Even if you don't legally tie the knot, living with someone for a number of years in some states constitutes a common-law marriage. A common-law marriage generally is one in which partners live together for a period of time and present themselves to friends, family, and the community as being married but not having had a legal marriage ceremony. In other words, in the eyes of the law you are treated the same as husband and wife.

The ins and outs of marital law are complex and not within the scope of this book. If you want to learn more, I highly recommend you contact a family law attorney in your geographic area to discuss your specific situation.

When you commit to another person romantically and live together as partners, there are financial ramifications. Whether you talk about money or not, you are joined financially. Therefore, it's best to discuss money and how you prefer to share in (or in some cases, not share in) your financial obligations from the beginning to avoid discomfort and conflict in the end.

Financial Togetherness

One of the first questions to consider is whether you will have joint or separate banking accounts. While the majority of adults in committed relationships combine their finances, some decide to keep separate accounts.[5] The reasons for keeping one's finances separate vary, ranging from wanting privacy to being embarrassed about past money mistakes to deciding that it's financially prudent to do so. For example, many blended families maintain individual accounts and pay for their respective children's expenses from this segregated money. A blended family is one where the partners have been married and divorced and have children from these previous relationships. The couple may also have biological children together. The reason many blended families don't comingle their finances is that it often is legally and financially advantageous to remain separate entities until any children reach the age of 18.

Generationally speaking, baby boomers are more likely to share all their money than younger generations.[6] Likewise, gay couples are more apt to financially operate independently. According to Suzanne Slater, LICSW, founder of Gifted Generations and an expert in advising same-sex couples, this is based on the fact that same-sex couples were formally barred from joint legal status:

> In an openly hostile social climate, many couples needed to present themselves as unrelated individuals, as protection from threats to their physical safety, employment status, and expulsion from their families of origin. Assets were held separately, bank accounts were in one person's name, and domestic financial responsibilities were divided up either equally or proportionately according to each partner's individual income. With the legalization of same-sex marriage, same-sex couples often feel safe enough to update previous (enforced) patterns of financial independence with their newfound opportunity to visibly blend financial assets. The result is rich variations of arrangements from one same-sex couple to another. It may make these couples feel safer and more entitled to blending more of their assets and obligations than in the past.[7]

What is the best decision for you and your partner? There is no right decision, as everyone's situation varies. But it is best if you consciously and mindfully discuss and make these decisions together. All too often, partners just fall into a pattern of earning money and paying bills without a conversation about how this works for each person individually and the couple as a unit.

My friend Melissa once told me that she and her husband of 18 years still paid bills as if they were roommates in college. They are parents of two teenagers in high school, have established careers, but have never gotten around to consciously deciding how to manage finances as a family. To date, this arrangement has worked for them. But as their children go off to college and they start planning for retirement, time will tell if it will continue to do so.

Taking time to talk with your partner about the when, where, how, and why of your financial life together is ideal. To help you begin this dialogue, here are a few questions to consider. Use these inquiries to guide your conversation about how you two want to set up your financial life now that you are committing to each other.

1. How much financial autonomy do you want in the relationship?
2. Is there a large income or wealth differential in your partnership? How might this impact how you pay for expenses and how you hold assets?
3. Do you or your partner have bad debts, such as past-due student loans or large outstanding credit card balances? If so, how do you feel about paying off debts that you didn't accrue?

4. Do you or your partner have a child from a previous relationship? If so, do you receive or pay alimony or palimony? How might this income, or these expenses, be impacted by joining your financial lives?

5. Has one of you filed for bankruptcy in the past? If so, how might this impact your ability to borrow money going forward?

6. How will you pay for household expenses? What seems to be equitable given your respective incomes?

7. What amount do you consider acceptable to spend without your partner's approval? Any amount or a set dollar limit?

8. How do you plan to file your tax returns, as individuals or as a married couple?

9. How did you handle money in past relationships and what did you learn from that experience?

10. Emotionally, what would it feel like to have separate versus joint bank accounts?

Many couples decide on the hybrid approach to their family finances. They have one joint account for household expenses, and two separate, individual accounts to use at each account holder's discretion. This allows partners to buy each other gifts, or spend money without always needing permission to do so. It can be the best of both worlds—being financially connected, with a healthy dose of autonomy.

There are many more financial conversations to be had when you are moving in with your partner, or getting married. (Even if you have been living together for years, having this conversation now can be helpful, as it is never too late to talk about finances.) Whether or not you want to combine your money is just one of them. But if you engage in this money talk it will help open the lines of communication in your partnership and make future money decisions a little easier.

Honey, I Want a Prenup

Historically, prenuptial agreements (prenups for short) were used to protect the estate of a wealthy man or woman who was marrying someone from a lower financial class. The idea was to protect the wealthier partner, and often their family, from a gold digger. Today, these agreements are not just for the rich, but often are suitable for many individuals. However, prenups have gotten bad press. Most people have money scripts that say if a partner wants a prenup, then there is no trust in the relationship and the marriage is doomed to fail. Like most money scripts, these thoughts are extreme and often untrue.

A prenuptial agreement is a document that summarizes how you will handle your finances during your marriage and in the event of a divorce. If you have children from a previous marriage or have significant assets or family wealth, prenuptial agreements protect your children and your wealth should your marriage end prior to your death.

Rick Kahler, a financial planner and author, wanted to have a prenuptial agreement in his second marriage based on what he learned in his first union. He and his fiancé met with a couples therapist to discuss his desire to protect his business assets in the event of a divorce. While the couple decided to forgo signing a prenup, Kahler found these conversations very useful. As he put it, "We had the hard discussions. We didn't sweep money and finances under the rug. Through the process, we educated each other about how we thought and felt about money, and I feel far better to have had the experience than not."

As a planner, Rick feels it's his obligation to bring up the topic of a prenuptial agreement with all his clients. Not only does he feel it is ethical to do so, he also believes the conversations that ensue build a foundation of mutual understanding in a marriage.

Signing a prenuptial agreement before you marry is a legal decision that you should consider and ultimately make with the guidance of an attorney and a financial advisor as there are many facets to these agreements that are outside the scope of this book. Often these agreements are signed when one partner owns a business, comes from family wealth, or has gone through a divorce and has children from a previous marriage. Protecting the children's inheritance, the family money, or your business entity is a sound financial decision. If one of these scenarios applies to your life and you are thinking about a prenup, consider these steps before approaching your partner.

Discuss Your Options with Your Attorney and/or Advisor

Know the legalities related to entering this type of agreement by consulting an expert in the field. Also include a financial expert in the conversation, since a large proportion of the documents relates to money matters, both in marriage and if you break up. It is often best to consult on these matters alone, before bringing your partner into the dialogue. One reason is that you may gather this information and then decide against putting a prenuptial agreement in place.

Consider How Your Partner May Emotionally Receive This Request

As with any difficult money talk, take time to consider how your request may feel to your fiancé. If this person comes from affluence and prenuptial agreements are routinely signed in their family, then being asked to sign one before marriage may not be a big deal to him or her. However, if your partner is not familiar with these documents, then you want to educate them about the financial reasons for having one while communicating that this is *not* a vote of no confidence in your relationship.

Determine an Emotionally Savvy Way to Broach the Topic

Being emotionally intelligent is key to the success in a prenuptial conversation. Approach your loved one with empathy and an understanding of how this may bring up difficult and complex feelings. Make sure you explain that while the conversations you want to engage in have a legal purpose, they will also help each of you understand the other person's money mindset and values.

According to James S. Sexton, a New York divorce trial lawyer, "It's all about timing. In the middle of a 'heated discussion' about finance? Don't throw the prenup into the mix right now." Instead Sexton recommends that you do some advance planning and select a time when you are "both in a positive frame of mind, when you have the time and energy for an in-depth discussion." Consider beginning the conversation by asking your partner about their expectations of how you two might save and manage student loan debt once you are married. In other words, ease into it. Don't just declare, "Honey, I want a prenup!"[8]

Consider a Professional Mediator to Facilitate These Conversations

Working with a neutral third party to facilitate this discussion is a good idea when you and your partner are considering a prenuptial agreement. Consider enlisting a couple or marital therapist, a financial advisor, a family wealth consultant, or a mediator in the process. At some point, you each will need to consult an attorney who will represent your individual interests when reviewing and signing the agreement. However, it is often best first to hash out the details of the arrangement with a professional trained in helping couples communicate about difficult topics more effectively.

Focus on More Than the Legalities

Every couple engaged to be married should discuss money. Talk honestly with your intended about how you plan to manage money once you are married. As part of this process, make sure you include conversations about money mindset, money histories, and shared and individual values and financial goals. If you have children, or plan to have a family, also discuss important money lessons you want to pass on to the next generation.

Whether you draft a prenuptial agreement or not, I strongly encourage you to have a series of premarital money talks. As with the decision about joint versus separate bank accounts, discussing other aspects of your future life together is warranted. Here are some topics to consider addressing.

- *Debt:* What debt do you currently have and what is the status of this debt? Do you have past-due loans, or outstanding credit card debt? If so, do you believe that you and your partner should pay that debt off together or is that your responsibility?

- *Real Estate:* What are your thoughts on buying versus renting a home? What does owning a home represent to you? What are you willing to give up, if anything, to buy a home?

- *Savings:* What is your philosophy when it comes to saving money? What were you taught about saving money growing up? How much do you currently have in your savings account(s)?

- *Spending:* What is your philosophy when it comes to spending money? What were you taught about spending money growing up? What are your thoughts about paying cash versus using a credit card when making purchases?

- *Philanthropy:* Do you believe in charitable giving? If so, what charities do you donate to? How much of your income do you believe you should give to others?

The more you can open the lines of communication at the beginning of your marriage, the better off you will be in the long run. Take the time and have a few money dates on your way to marital bliss.

Breaking Up Is Hard to Do

The odds of a couple splitting up are pretty high in the United States, with 50 percent of first marriages, and 67 percent of second marriages, ending in divorce.[9] It is a myth that the longer you are married the more likely you are to stay together, as more than 28 percent of divorcees in the United States are now age 50 or older.[10] With same-sex marriage now legal in all fifty states, we can eventually expect more same-sex divorces to follow.

You may have walked down the aisle on your wedding day thinking your love could endure anything, but in reality, only half of couples grow old and die together. This statistic alone can make a good case for a prenuptial agreement. But many couples don't have one in place, and are forced to have one of the most difficult money conversations of their lives, often at a time when they really don't even like each other.

"How do we split of up our assets?" is a charged question. Even in the best of circumstances, deciding who gets what after spending time together is challenging. As one divorcee noted, "If you approach the conversation with love and friendship, it goes much more smoothly than when you just want to stick it to the other person." Of course, this is easier if the breakup was mutually agreed upon, or there are no children, so custody issues are removed from the equation.

While financial tension doesn't cause a marriage to break up, it can contribute to or exacerbate existing problems in the relationship that ultimately undermine the union. As discussed in Chapter 1, money and how you use it often symbolizes love, trust, respect, control, power, and self-worth. Often money arguments are about so much more than finances. For example, Pilar's ex-husband Peter often withheld financial resources from her when he was angry. As a stay-at-home mom with two small children, she didn't earn an income and was dependent on Peter financially. Peter drank too much and felt inadequate deep down. While Pilar blames their financial woes on the breakup of their marriage, one could say that it was Peter's depression and alcoholism, combined with her codependency, that hurt the marriage. Yes, Peter withheld money to feel powerful and important, and his wife tried to spend less to make him happy. But money wasn't the root of the problem; it was just a sign of their struggles.

Now flash forward to Pilar and Peter discussing the best way to split up their assets and care for their children. Because they used money as a scapegoat during their entire marriage, they both hire lawyers who argue endlessly about the financial assets. Again, Peter is trying to win and feel powerful, and Pilar is acquiescing and trying to please. Needless to say, neither one is on their best behavior.

Pilar and Peter's divorce may be an extreme example. But if you have gone through a divorce, or watched your parents break up, you probably can identify with parts of their story, in which money became the weapon. You can avoid such a situation, or at least reduce the likelihood of it happening, if you consider some of these suggestions.

Consider Working with a Therapist

Going through a divorce is a very emotional life transition. Most, if not all, people who go through a split feel like they failed, and question their past decisions. Working with a therapist can help you process your feelings about the divorce and help you develop coping strategies for dealing with this turbulent time. You need to make many financial decisions during a divorce, so having a safe place to talk about your feelings is a great way to prevent these emotions from dictating your financial future.

Consult with a Financial Advisor

If you have a financial advisor who works with you as a couple, talk to this professional about the best course of action going forward now that you and your partner have decided to break up. It is probably in both your best interests to not continue working with the same advisor. Ask for a referral and decide if one or both of you will hire a new advisor. If you don't work with an advisor, now is a good time to connect with one. There are advisors who specialize in divorce and can educate you on the many financial decisions you will need to make. Divorce is a topic unto itself with many of these decisions outside the realm of this book. A big part of divorce is about separating your marital assets in an equitable fashion. Therefore, working with a financial expert is a prudent way to make sure you are taken care of when the marriage dissolves.

Contemplate Mediation

The couples that typically end up less emotionally scarred by a divorce went to a mediator before they hired an attorney. (See Sidebar 7.1, Know Your Divorce Options.) Couples hire a mediator to help them decide how to fairly divide their assets. If children are involved, then the mediator also works with the partners to design a mutually agreeable child custody agreement. This option is less adversarial than litigation, and it is less costly.

"The common idea most couples have is that they will act like adults during a divorce," says financial planner Rick Kahler. "The belief is we will do this amicably. Typically, at some point in the process, the couples go off the rails. Often this is when the lawyers get involved." Remember that a divorce attorney's client is the individual and the attorney has a responsibility to advocate for the best outcome for their client. This stance lends itself to a you-against-me dynamic that brings with it intense and sometimes damaging feelings.

SIDEBAR 7.1 KNOW YOUR DIVORCE OPTIONS

Litigation: Involves both parties hiring legal counsel and going through the traditional court system to dissolve the marriage. This is the most costly option.

Collaborative Divorce: You agree to work out a divorce settlement without going to court. This method involves you and your partner and your respective attorneys consenting to work toward a mutually agreeable settlement. This option often involves using a divorce financial advisor as a neutral party to determine an equitable settlement, as well as a coach or financial therapist to help facilitate conversations regarding child custody and other emotionally laden topics.

Mediation: You and your partner work with a neutral mediator who helps both of you come to an agreement on all aspects of dissolving your marriage, including dividing the financial assets. This is the least costly option, as legal counsel is only involved once an agreement is reached.

Know That This May Not Be Your Last Money Talk

When you have children, it is important to remember that the divorce settlement will not be your last financial conversation with your former spouse. Depending on the ages of your children, you will be communicating with your ex-spouse for years to come about how to pay for child-related expenses. Therefore, maintaining a respectful and civil tone is helpful in setting the stage for future money talks. You may not like your soon-to-be ex very much in the moment, but holding on to the idea that you are a role model of financial communication skills to your children may just help you stay calm when you feel like lashing out.

Divorce is not easy, no matter what the circumstances. It may be one of the most difficult money talks of your life. But you don't have to go it alone. Enlist help and remember that if you can get through this financial conversation, the rest will be easier.

Until Death Does Us Part

No one likes to think about death. We all know that one day we will have to say goodbye to those we love, but we push that thought out of our heads. Who wants to spend time talking to your partner about dying, when you can drink wine and enjoy the here and now? Yes, talking about death is almost as taboo as talking about money. Put the two topics together and you have one big elephant in the room that no one wants to discuss. The problem is that if you ignore this fact of life now, you are inadvertently setting up your loved one for pain later.

Ask my friend Cori, who suddenly lost her husband Tim when she was 58 years old. One day she was married with two adult children, the next she was widowed with a financial mess to cope with. A few months before Tim's heart attack, he had canceled his life insurance policy to catch up on some past-due bills. Cori had no idea he had done this. "I was so angry at him. First he died on me. Then he left me without any financial security. Why would he make such a stupid decision?"

Cori will never know the answer. But she does know the importance of talking about these matters with her adult children. "I don't ever want my girls to have to worry about how they will pay for their husband's funeral like I did."

Losing a spouse or partner is difficult enough without having to worry about the finances. While most adults intellectually appreciate the need to plan, few take action. Only 34 percent of adults in the United States have drafted a will, even though 69 percent of adults have considered it.[11] However, the taboo against talking about and planning for death can be broken, just like the money talk taboo.

National Public Radio aired a story about a town where everyone talks about death. The town is La Crosse, Wisconsin, where 96 percent of people die with an advance directive or similar documentation in place.[12] An advance directive is a written document that indicates a person's wishes for their medical treatment should that person be unable to communicate their wishes to the doctor. One type of advance directive, a living will, is used when a person is terminally ill, and unable to make their own medical or healthcare decisions. What's fascinating about La Crosse is that instead of there being peer pressure to avoid conversations about death, there is actually societal pressure to make estate plans and communicate them to your loved ones and neighbors.

It all started with one man, Bud Hammes, the medical ethicist working at the local hospital. He decided that his job helping families make life-and-death decisions would be easier if families had already had a conversation about their end-of-life wishes well before the crisis. Bud decided to teach nurses and the medical staff how to coach patients and community members on how to have these difficult but important conversations. Bud was successful, and now it is taboo in La Crosse to *not* have an advance directive and estate documents in place.[13]

My hope is something similar happens with the money taboo, and the inclination against talking about money goes out of fashion soon. Until it does, you must take the initiative to draft your estate plan and then communicate the specifics to your children and loved ones. This money talk is commonly referred to as a legacy conversation. The purpose of this conversation is to let your children or beneficiaries know your wishes, to explain to them the documents that are in your estate plan, and to answer any questions they may have about your wishes.

SIDEBAR 7.2 BASIC ESTATE PLANNING DOCUMENTS

Estate plans vary in terms of complexity, but usually include the following documents at a minimum:

Will/Trust: Document that tells the court who will receive your assets in the event of your death. If you have minor children, it assigns individual(s) to be their guardians.

Durable Power of Attorney: Document that designates a person to enter into legal and financial transactions on your behalf if you are unable to do so yourself.

Healthcare Power of Attorney: Document that designates another individual, often a spouse or family member, to make important healthcare decisions on your behalf in the event of incapacity.

Healthcare Directives: Written statement specifying your end-of-life wishes. This may include a living will, a do-not-resuscitate (DNR) order, or other wishes you determine are important.

To determine your estate planning needs, contact an attorney in your area. To find a referral, ask a trusted friend, your bank, or your financial advisor.

By this point, you may be thinking sarcastically, "Wow, this sounds like a ton of fun!" Well, it is not all gloom and doom. Part of a healthy legacy conversation is a dialogue about your core values, your financial successes, and what your family means to you. These money talks can be very rewarding and healing, and bring partners and families closer together.

Rebecca's mom didn't wait until she was ill to discuss her estate plan with her daughters. "One day she just showed up with a big box of paperwork and started telling my sister and me about her finances and where her passwords were kept. I asked her what prompted this spontaneous discussion and she said, 'I read an article in the newspaper that told me I should do this.'" Since that initial meeting, Rebecca's family has had many more such conversations and she is glad, as she feels they have allowed her to understand her mother better.

Sharing your estate plan and end-of-life wishes with your adult children is really a way of letting them know more about what you care about and what is important for them to remember. While the dialogue may start because of the unpleasant reality that there will come a day when someone you love will die, these conversations end up being about so much more.

Take the Lead in Talking about Your Legacy

Why not give your adult children the gift of sharing your thoughts and beliefs about when, where, and how you would like to be cared for as you age? Instead of waiting until you are physically or mentally slowing down, be proactive and invite your adult children to plan with you, to ask questions about your future financial and emotional needs, and put their minds at ease.

Discussing end-of-life issues is uncomfortable for most of us. But it is a necessary money conversation. The best time to engage in this dialogue with your family is when you are healthy and the days where you will need support seem far away. The challenge is that your motivation may be lower when a crisis is not looming. The advantage is that you can be proactive, not reactive. Your adult children will be relieved that the burden of raising this topic has not fallen on them. If you are an adult child and your parents have not raised this topic, then read Chapter 9, where you will learn how to have this money talk.

Keep a few things in mind as you prepare for this conversation. The first is don't procrastinate. It always seems like there is plenty of time to decide how to fund your healthcare as you age and what type of help you prefer, until time runs out. Just ask Kiefer, whose family wanted to proactively plan, but his father insisted that he "would never need a nurse or help." When he had complications during a surgical procedure, the family was left scrambling to make decisions and get him the care he needed. As Kiefer said, "It would have been much better had his pride not interfered and he let us help ahead of time."

Kiefer's family did find a suitable place for his dad's care, but then had the additional worry about how to pay for it. "It worked out in the end, but ended up being a very stressful few weeks."

It's easy to avoid facing our mortality and talking about our inevitable physical decline. It is tempting to think optimistically or ignore the reality of our humanness, but doing so often leaves the ones we care for most in a very stressful position. Fight the urge to procrastinate. Instead, open up the dialogue with your partner, and then your children. While these money talks can be uncomfortable at first, they can actually make a family stronger.

Once you decide to engage in the conversation, it's time to do some soul searching. Ponder questions such as:

1.   What is important to me as I age? What values do I want to honor in my senior years? What legacy do I want to leave behind?

2. What type of health and senior care is important to me? Is it being cared for at home, or being cared for in a way that preserves my dignity and safety?

3. Is it imperative that my caregiver is a family member, or simply someone trustworthy who becomes an important part of the family?

4. How do I plan to pay for my health and senior care and who can help me execute this plan if I become unable to do so myself?

5. How can I communicate my wishes and my values to the next generation?

Today there are various medical and housing options available should you become mentally or physically impaired. These include home health-care, assisted living facilities, rehabilitation units, day care programs, and nursing homes. Discussing these options and your preferences with your partner and children will ease their minds if and when the time comes to implement the plan.

When discussing your healthcare wishes, don't ask your adult children to make promises that they may not be able to keep. During the initial discussion, it may be easy for your children to agree to keep you out of a nursing home or to act as your primary caregiver if you become ill. But this option may not be in anyone's best interest in the long run. Avoid asking family members to make these types of promises. Instead, talk about what is underneath your request. For example, if you are tempted to want them to promise to keep you at home, consider your motivations. Is it the fear of being abandoned and the belief that if you are at home you won't be? If so, then communicate how you feel: "I am concerned that as I age I will be forgotten about. While I prefer to stay at home, I know that the future is uncertain and that may not make sense at the time. Just know that what is most important to me is that people visit me as I age." By being clear and direct, your family can do its best to honor your requests and still provide you with the best care possible when the need arises.

There is a legal and logistical part to every legacy conversation. This includes reviewing your estate plan with the next generation and discussing the purpose of each document with them. (Refer to Sidebar 7.2, Basic Estate Planning Documents, for additional information.) Let your adult children or your beneficiaries know where these papers are kept so they can be easily assessed during an emergency. Having this knowledge helps reduce their stress at difficult times, and helps ensure that you get the care you requested. It is also a good idea to give a copy of any of your healthcare documents to your primary care doctor so there is a copy in your medical file.

Gwen Morgan, the author of the *What if . . .* Workbook, knows firsthand the value of legacy conversations. She wrote her book after experiencing a few personal losses and realizing the power of having a legacy conversation before a loved one dies. Gwen explains, "My mother was only seventy years young when she passed. I remember as we planned my mother's funeral there was disagreement among my family members on various issues, like which dress to lay her out in and what type of music to have. There are so many decisions to make. And in the midst of it all, you are mourning the loss of a beloved person in your life."[14] Four years later, Gwen's Aunt Jeannette died and her cousin Michelle seemed very calm at the funeral. When Gwen asked her how she was doing, Michelle explained that her mother had written down everything she wanted, from what dress she wanted to be laid out in to her instructions that she be buried with her bible and her rosary. Knowing what was important to her mother allowed Michelle to focus on grieving without having to second-guess all these decisions. Gwen realized that this was a gift her Aunt Jeannette had given her family and the idea for the *What if . . .* Workbook was born.

A few years later when Gwen realized it was time to discuss estate planning with her father, she drafted the first copy of the Workbook. She used checklists and questionnaires as a way for her father to communicate important financial information and end-of-life wishes to her and her brother. A private man, Gwen's father didn't want to talk with his adult children about these matters, but he was willing to write his thoughts down on paper. Ultimately, this process helped the family communicate about these sensitive topics and provided each of them with the peace of mind that when the time came, they had discussed these issues.

Legacy conversations are not one-time events. They are ongoing dialogues that change as you and your family members age. While it may be challenging to begin this discussion, families who take the risk to break the money silence around death and dying often find great comfort in having shared their thoughts and feelings with each other before it was too late.

Summary

In this chapter, you learned the value of engaging in difficult money talks with your partner and your family.

- When you romantically commit, you are entering a financial partnership.
- Emotional intelligence plays a key role in handling challenging financial conversations successfully.

- You know what questions to consider as you merge your money with a partner's.
- You've learned five things to consider when you are breaking up your marriage and your assets.
- You understand the importance of estate planning and communicating your wishes to the next generation.

Money Talk Challenge: Preparing for a Legacy Conversation

Preparing for potentially difficult or uncomfortable money talks is the key to a successful outcome. Below is a series of questions to help you prepare for a legacy conversation. If you have children, consider how you might use these questions to communicate your wishes to them. If you don't have children, think about who you want to leave your legacy to and then use these inquiries accordingly. It is okay if you don't have all the answers now. The goal is to simply start to consider your responses so you can eventually give your family the gift of knowing your wishes.

1. Your Success Story

   a. What is your personal or family success story, and how does this story express your core values?

   b. What are the financial lessons embedded in this story?

   c. What other family stories may be helpful to communicate to your family? These may include successes, but also mistakes and lessons learned.

2. Your Core Values

   a. What are the three most important personal or family values you want to pass down to the next generation?

   b. What makes these values important to you?

   c. What stories or examples from your own life may help communicate these values to your heirs?

3. Your Charitable Giving

   a. How do you view philanthropy and charitable giving as part of your legacy?

   b. What charitable organizations do you currently give to and what organizations might you include in your estate plan?

   c. What type of gifts (include financial and non-financial) would you like to give the next generation and when do you plan to gift them?

4.   Your Business (*for business owners only*)

   a.   Do you have a business succession plan? If not, what is your rationale for not having one? If you do have one, what did you learn in the process of developing it?

   b.   Who will inherit the business, or will you sell your business? Is there a buy-sell agreement in place and if not, when will that be drafted?

   c.   Have you communicated your intentions to your family and key stakeholders? Why or why not?

5.   Your Estate Plan

   a.   Do you have a will and/or an estate plan? If so, has it been reviewed in the last year? If not, when do you plan to draft one?

   b.   Have you shared your end-of-life wishes and health directives with the next generation?

   c.   If not, when do you plan to have this conversation? Who can you enlist to help facilitate this dialogue?

For Advisors

Answer the questions above for yourself. Advisors are people too, and even though you are in the field, you may not have set up your own estate plan, or if applicable, put your buy-sell agreement in place. It is important to model healthy planning for your clients.

Next, consider using this activity with your clients as a way to begin these sometimes difficult conversations. Be a resource to your clients and their children. It is a great way to foster trust and it is a natural way to meet, and hopefully eventually work with, the next generation.

CHAPTER EIGHT

Kids and Money Talk: Raising a Financially Intelligent Next Generation

Raising children is a creative endeavor, an art rather than a science.
—Bruno Bettelheim, 20th-century child psychologist

Learning to ski is a rite of passage in my family, so everyone was excited when my youngest nephew, Garrett, was old enough to join us for a day on the mountain. He was seven years old at the time and very excited to go skiing with his grandfather, aunt, uncle, and older brother. On the way to the ski resort, my father stopped at a local ski shop to rent Garrett equipment to use for the day. The intent was to rent him skis, boots, and poles, but once in the ski shop Garrett declared that he wanted to snowboard. Without thinking, my father fitted him for a snowboard and boots. An hour later, we were standing at the top of the North Star Trail at Sugarbush Resort, staring at each other and suddenly wondering who would teach Garrett how to snowboard. All of us were skiers. Garrett wanted to snowboard and had the right equipment, but no one in the family knew how to snowboard. Brian and I burst out laughing as my father looked down at Garrett and declared that he was taking him back to the ski shop to rent skis. We just weren't capable of teaching him a skill that none of us possessed.

Later that day, Garrett learned to ski. Each of us took turns sharing our nuggets of wisdom. My father taught him how to turn by putting his skis in the shape of a pizza slice and putting pressure on the downhill edge. Brian showed him how to get on and off the chair lift and I taught him how to get up when he fell down. Garrett took to the sport and is an avid alpine skier to this day.

As a parent or a loving relative or mentor to a young person, you can only teach what you know. If you were raised in money silence, then it is challenging (but not impossible) to empower your children to talk about money and be financially intelligent. Remember, *financial intelligence* is defined as having financial knowledge and skills, as well as insight into your relationship with money. Someone who is truly financially intelligent understands the mechanics of personal finance as well as the emotional aspects of managing money. To raise a financially fit next generation, you may need to learn a few new things. But the effort will be worth it, if it means that your kids and their kids will live richer lives.

My family would have loved to teach Garrett how to snowboard. But to do so, one of us would have had to take lessons or enlist a snowboard instructor to teach him. Trust me, if we thought Garrett needed to master this skill to live a productive and responsible adult life, we would have invested the time and money. But winter sports are not a make-it-or-break-it skill set. Knowing how to earn, manage, and discuss money is vital to the well-being of your children and the young people in your life.

Teaching the next generation about money is as important as teaching them how to eat nutritiously, exercise regularly, and find their life purpose. Unfortunately, schools in the United States don't share this view. As of the writing of this book, only 17 states require high school students to take a course in personal finance.[1] The remaining 33 states do not consider teaching the next generation basic money skills a priority. It seems that most states require students from elementary school through high school to participate in physical education, but they don't mandate that they also become financially fit.[2]

The bottom line: it is up to you—the parent, aunt, uncle, or grandparent—to empower the next generation to be financially savvy. You are a role model for earning, managing, and talking about money. The good news is that teaching kids about money can be fun and strengthen family bonds. And you may just increase your financial intelligence along the way.

In this chapter, you will learn how to be a role model for healthy financial habits and how to talk about money with children. If you don't have kids of your own, you can apply these lessons to any young person in your life. As they say, "It takes a village," and that is true when it comes to breaking money silence with the next generation.

Look, Mom and Dad, You're a Role Model!

Being a parent is a difficult job. There are so many lessons to impart to your children. Don't do drugs. Eat your peas. Be kind to others. Practice safe sex. The list goes on and on. Finding time to teach your children about money, especially if it's not a subject you are comfortable with, can be daunting. But like it or not, if you are a parent, you are a primary financial role model. In fact, according to a survey conducted by U.S. Bank, 91 percent of college-aged students say they learned their financial habits from their parents.[3]

The good news is that you have influence over your kids! The more troubling news is that collectively, parents are not doing a very good job teaching the next generation how to be financially intelligent. According to the U.S. Bank survey, only 19 percent of the students reported having parents who taught them specific ways to manage money. About half of the students acquired general financial knowledge from their mom and dad. Twenty-one percent learned only through example, and 9 percent were not taught how to manage money at all.[4]

Parents have a lot of power to shape the next generation's money mind-sets and teach them to talk openly about money. But money silence is blocking them from using their influence. The millennial generation is repeating mistakes made by previous generations, such as spending too much and saving too little. In fact, 44 percent of the students surveyed by U.S. Bank said they "have little or no knowledge on creating and keeping a budget."[5] Developing spending plans and tracking expenses are rudimentary financial skills, but somehow, we are not teaching our children the basics.

Joan, a retired high school math teacher and mother of three adult children, shared this insight: "When I was young, you learned personal finance through osmosis. Your parents showed you how to balance a checkbook, create a budget, and start a savings account at your local bank. As a teacher, I realized that young people weren't learning about finance through osmosis. Parents weren't taking the time to teach their children about money. Many parents didn't understand finance themselves."

Joan realized that students weren't receiving adequate financial literacy training at home, so she created a personal finance course for high school juniors and seniors. She used experiential learning to motivate these young adults to see how these lessons applied to their lives currently and invited guest speakers in on a variety of topics. The students and parents loved the course and praised it as "one of the high school classes that really meant something to me—I am really using it." When Joan retired, the course was absorbed into a basic math class in a watered-down version. Without a state mandate to incorporate financial literacy into the high school curriculum, this course went by the wayside.

Part of the challenge for parents is that money management is not as straightforward as it was in the past. As Joan notes, "Things were simpler. We didn't have credit cards when I was younger. My dad taught me how to balance a checkbook. When I went off to college, I opened a checking account and paid for everything by check." Now, young people have credit cards, debit cards, and online payment accounts. Their money is not managed in one centralized place and it becomes easier to lose track of spending. Each of these purchasing options comes with different interest rates and fees. Adding student loans to the mix brings another layer of complexity to personal money management. It is challenging for parents to keep up with all these changes, let alone teach another person how to navigate these choices.[6]

Beyond the increased complexity of personal finance, there are additional roadblocks parents encounter when it comes to raising financially intelligent children. Many of these are based on the myth that talking about money with loved ones is taboo. According to the 2016 T. Rowe Price "Parents, Kids, and Money Survey," 72 percent of parents experience "at least some reluctance to talk to their kids about financial matters."[7] The reasons for their apprehension vary, but it all seems to boil down to the money silence in our society. Let's look at the top five reasons adults are reluctant to discuss money matters with children.

I Don't Want My Kids to Worry

Fifty-two percent of parents say the reason they didn't talk to their children about money is they don't want their kids to worry, according to the T. Rowe Price survey.[8] While I can appreciate not wanting to unduly worry your children, I do think this is an excuse for continuing money silence. Little ones are perceptive and they often pick up on unspoken feelings in a home. You may think your silence is protecting them, when in fact it is fueling their concern.

Of course, I am not recommending that you discuss your fears about your business failing with your seven-year-old son or your anxiety about getting laid off from your job with your 12-year-old daughter. But I do believe it is a good practice to share your thoughts and feelings about the money decisions you make for the family. For example, if you need to replace the car muffler, talk with your children about the short-term sacrifices you need to make to pay for this unexpected expense. Or if your year-end bonus check was much less than you anticipated, explain why going out to dinner more than once a month may not be prudent for a while. These are all important opportunities to teach young people how to make wise financial decisions.

My Kids Are Too Young to Understand

Thirty-six percent of parents answering the T. Rowe Price survey stated that money talks don't happen in their homes because their kids are too young to understand finance.[9] I respectfully disagree. It is never too early to start teaching your children about money and engaging them in financial conversations. (For more information, see Tip #1 later in this chapter.) Doing so early introduces the notion that talking about money is acceptable and necessary. Not including children in financial conversations sends a powerful message that money talk should be avoided or is shameful to participate in. Most financial literacy experts agree that the best age to start discussing money with your kids is age five, as this is when little ones become aware of money.

Yes, parents need to adjust the complexity of the conversation to match their child's developmental stage. But don't use this as an excuse to skip money talk altogether. If you do find yourself using this as a reason, then take some time to wonder where this belief originated and how it may not serve the next generation of your family.

I Would Rather Discuss Other Important Matters

A quarter of parents in the T. Rowe Price survey indicated that they would rather discuss other important things with their children instead of financial matters.[10] As I indicated earlier, parents do have a heavy burden when it comes to teaching their children about life. But learning basic money skills is vital. Personal finance is a big part of adult life. Think about the last time you went through an entire day and didn't have to make a financial decision or use money to pay for a purchase. My guess is that this rarely happens.

It seems that parents in this category have bought into the notion that money talk is taboo, so they shouldn't discuss it with children at all. If you were raised with this family money message, then it makes sense. But again, the lack of financial skills training is hurting young people, and you can't rely on the schools to teach it. If you find that you have too many other important topics to discuss with your kids, then incorporate money lessons into these conversations. For example, if you are educating your children about being active and living a healthy life, discuss the costs associated with these activities. Educate them on how investing money in self-care now pays good dividends in the future. Money conversations don't have to be separate from other life lessons; they can be easily included in the discussions you are already having as a family.

I Don't Want My Kids to Share Our Secrets with Others

Twenty-three percent of parents in the T. Rowe Price survey said their rationale for not talking to their kids about family finances is the fear that their children will share sensitive financial information with friends and neighbors.[11] Bull's-eye! Kids are too young and inexperienced to understand that money is a taboo topic. How refreshing it is that they may feel comfortable discussing money with anyone—even someone outside of their own home. While I appreciate that some financial data should remain private, this parental fear primarily stems from adults' discomfort with talking about money, not necessarily their kids' inability to keep a secret. Besides, most of the information that they might share is only a mouse-click away. A simple Google search with your name, age, and address yields an abundance of data, ranging from how much you paid for your home to the traffic ticket you received last year when you were running late to the office.

When you are talking with your kids about money matters, tailor the information you share based on their age and maturity level. For example, you may find it helpful to show your 15-year-old daughter your year-end Roth IRA statement so she can learn about saving for the future. But you don't have to share all the information about your investment portfolio. In any money talk, you are the adult and you decide what to divulge and what to keep close to the vest.

If you are concerned that others will find out about your financial situation, take some time to ponder where this worry stems from. Is this a valid concern or an old money script that no longer serves you? How might you teach your kids how to have good boundaries around sensitive information but at the same time feel comfortable discussing some money matters with those outside the family? This may be a tricky balance to achieve. But the effort is worthwhile, as it will help them feel more comfortable engaging in money talk in general.

It's None of Their Business

A little over 10 percent of parents answering the T. Rowe Price survey indicated that financial matters are for adults only. In other words, finances are none of my kids' business.[12] When I hear this excuse, I picture a 70-year-old man who was socialized to believe that he was solely responsible for providing for the family and that children are to be seen and not heard. But this survey was done with parents primarily in their mid-thirties to fifties. It seems that they too have been socialized to believe wholeheartedly in perpetuating money silence in their families.

My husband Brian grew up in a family that abided by this belief. He never learned how to pay bills, write a check, or pay taxes. As a result, he made some financial mistakes in his early twenties. Co-signing on a friend's loan that later went into default without his knowledge ruined his credit. He bounced checks without realizing the high price of this habit. Eventually, Brian did learn how to manage money, but only after these painful lessons. Now, he is passionate about breaking money silence because he knows firsthand the challenges of not being taught about finances as a kid.

When you review these top five reasons parents are hesitant to discuss financial matters with their children, it all boils down to one underlying belief—money talk is taboo. But the costs of not proactively talking about money are serious for the next generation. If you are reading this book, then my guess is you agree these costs are too high.

Later in this chapter, you will learn 10 tips for raising financially intelligent kids. But first, let's look at how the media influences your child's money mindset, especially if you remain silent.

The Power of the Media

One of the scariest parts about parents being quiet when it comes to money matters is that they are letting advertisers and media companies control the financial conversation. Your kids hear messages of conspicuous consumption and materialism over and over again, because repetition is a key strategy for advertisers looking to sell products. Unless you interject your family values into the conversation, your kids might just adopt an unhealthy money mindset.

Here are some statistics that I think you should know about how advertisers using online, television, and print media influence your children's money mindset without your permission.

- Seventeen billion dollars is spent annually to market to children.[13]
- Children under age 12 influence five hundred *billion* in purchases annually.[14]

- Seventy-one percent of children ages 8 to 18 have televisions in their bedrooms.[15]
- Children ages 2 to 11 view on average 25,600 television advertisements a year.[16]
- Teens ages 13 to 17 engage in brand-related conversations approximately 145 times a week.[17]

These statistics speak volumes. As a concerned parent or family member, you may be reluctant to engage in money talk with kids, but it is necessary if you want to combat the daily stream of messages the next generation receives online, on television, and in social media. You need to make your voice as strong as, if not stronger than, marketers who want to sell your kids a product.

Sam X Renick, the founder of SammyRabbit.com, a financial literacy program for elementary students, says, "Parents really need to take charge of the money conversation. Advertisers use repetition to send their messages. Moms and dads, as well as teachers, need to compete with these messages and use repetition with young people too."[18]

Renick's philosophy of using mantras to teach young people how to save and spend responsibly stems from how Sam's father taught him about finance. "My dad came up with a lot of slogans. He'd post them in the bathroom on the mirror and various places throughout the house. 'You can have anything you want if you are willing to work for it.' He must've repeated that to me maybe ten thousand different times throughout my childhood and teenage life." Other messages included "saving is a great habit" and "pay yourself first." Sam's dad repeated these themes using stories, songs, and written slogans. This repetition helped Sam and his siblings develop a healthy relationship with money, even though they grew up with very little. Ultimately, these mantras morphed into the SammyRabbit.com program.[19]

"Parents give off a lot of messages that relate to money," says Renick. "They may not use the word 'money' in the sentence or the conversation, but it does imply something about money and typically it's [about] spending. So if you say to your kids you are going on a family vacation to Disneyland, then you are having a $500 to $2000 money conversation with them." His advice is to include the children in the conversation about how as a family you all will pay for this trip. Let them know that the family needs to save a certain amount each week or month so they can afford to go on vacation. Then include the kids in that process. Depending on their ages, have them save along with you. For example, a young child could collect returnable bottles and cans and then contribute the money they made recycling them at the grocery store. Or if a child is older and working, maybe have them contribute ten percent of their paycheck to a fun account to be used while they are traveling. Saving as a family is a great way to teach children healthy financial habits and for them to experience the rewards of their efforts.[20]

Another way to combat the effects of the media on your children's money mindset is to teach them how to be a critical media viewer, or media-literate. Media literacy is defined as having the ability to assess, analyze, evaluate, and create media. People who are media-literate can understand the complex messages embedded in print and online mediums such as books, commercials, the internet, movies, newspapers, television programs, and video games. Teaching kids this skill helps them decipher the verbal, nonverbal, and visual messages contained in media and then use critical thinking to decide if, when, and how to apply these lessons in their lives.

I wonder whether the large majority of parents who are reluctant to talk with their children about financial matters would be so hesitant if they truly understood the potential price of their silence. My guess is if you were ambivalent about having these conversations with your kids, you are now on board and ready to learn how to teach the next generation how to be financially intelligent.

Ten Tips for Teaching Financial Intelligence

When it comes to teaching children how to be financially intelligent, you'll find it helpful to consider the following tips. Every child and family situation is unique, so tailor these ideas to meet your family's needs. If you are an advisor working with clients around this topic, feel free to share these guidelines as a way to begin a dialogue around assisting the next generation in successfully managing wealth and living a financially fit life.

Tip #1: It Is Never Too Early or Too Late

I am often asked, "What is the best age to start talking to my children about money?" My answer is always, "It is never too early to start." Financial literacy experts encourage parents to begin money conversations when a child is between ages five and six, and then continue the dialogue over the child's lifetime. If your child is 15 and you have not started this type of education, remember it is never too late to break money silence with another person.

When I interviewed women and couples for my previous books (*How to Give Financial Advice to Women* and *How to Give Financial Advice to Couples*), I was surprised when some of my interviewees said it was "too late" to teach their children about money. These parents had children in their late teens or early twenties. It saddened me to think that a parent would give up on being a financial mentor simply because their children were approaching or in adulthood. Most of these interviewees felt a sense of disappointment for not being more proactive about financial literacy when their children were younger. When I told them it was not too late, some of them just laughed. Others started to consider how they could broach the subject given their kids' ages.

Money silence has a way of letting us off the hook, or allowing us to think it is too late to open the dialogue about personal finances as a family. The truth is, it is never too late to teach your kids about money. In a perfect world, every parent would impart financial lessons to their children between the ages of 5 and 15 as the experts recommend. But life is flawed and complicated. You may not have been given a roadmap on how to handle your own finances, so it becomes a challenge to teach your children how to do it well. But by reading this book, you now know that you can create a blueprint for family money conversations at any time in your child's life.

Stop thinking you have missed the boat and using this as an excuse to continue money silence with your kids. Instead, consider how to start the conversation. One way is to put words to the actions you modeled when your children were younger. For example, if you were a newly divorced mom when your child was in elementary school and you were stressed out every time you paid bills, ask your adult children what that experience was like for them. Explain that paying bills was new for you, as their father had done this when you were married. Then ask them what they noticed when they were younger. Talk with them about the mistakes you made with money, as well as your financial successes. Take the opportunity today and learn together.

Tip #2: Keep the Lessons Age-Appropriate

Financial literacy training needs to be age-appropriate. Teaching a five-year-old child about interest rate risk, hedge funds, or the global economy does not make sense. Children this age do not have the ability to think abstractly (which these concepts require), and these concepts are not applicable to their lives. Instead, starting around age five, teach a young child the names of coins and their corresponding monetary values.

Around age seven, have them practice making change and introduce them to the notion of *wants* versus *needs*. This is also a good age to introduce the idea of philanthropy. Find out what your children care about and why. Next, find a charity tied to this cause and help your child make periodic donations. This activity can be as simple as putting a percentage of the child's monetary gifts into a special piggy bank for this reason.

As your children age, the complexity of the lessons will grow. During the teen years, your child may decide to hold a fundraiser at his high school and donate the money to a worthy cause. The relevant tasks for him to handle would include identifying the charitable organization to donate to, recruiting peers to help, marketing the fundraiser, and then donating the money collected after expenses. The underlying philanthropic lesson is the same one you taught your child when he was younger, but the more sophisticated process of fundraising for and donating to a good cause reflects his increased knowledge and maturity level.

Tip#3: Be Consistent and Repeat Important Lessons over Time

Teach money lessons consistently over time and tie these activities to the young person's social and emotional development. Some concepts will be repeated over time, and some new ones will be introduced along the way. For example, an eight-year-old girl interested in starting a dog-walking service in the neighborhood can learn how to set a price for her services, how to collect money from her customers, and learn the value of hard work. A 16-year-old girl starting a similar dog-walking service can also learn these important money skills; however, she may also be ready to tackle accepting credit card payments and using a financial software program to manage cash flow.

Repeating basic money lessons over time reinforces key concepts and gives your children a chance to practice mastering these skills on their own. Remember that advertisers use repetition all the time to communicate with children and teens, so it's important that you use the same tactic as a way to cut through the noise.

Tip #4: It's Not Just about Dollars and Cents

Communicating your core values and showing kids how to express these values through their financial habits is as big a part of financial intelligence as teaching them about dollars and cents. If you grew up in a working-class environment, your parents may not have focused explicitly on sharing their values with you because they were busy earning a living.

If you grew up with affluence, money talk may have been discouraged as impolite and this type of conversation was sparse. Either way, discussing why and how you spend, save, invest, and give money is a very useful lesson. Your kids will pick up some of these messages along the way, but don't leave it up to chance. Talk about it.

Other non-financial lessons that are important to teach your children include mastering the art of delayed gratification, understanding and learning from your financial mistakes, and appreciating that reaching a long-term goal may involve short-term struggles. All these lessons increase your child's insight into their relationship with money and help them develop the emotional intelligence needed to be financially responsible.

Tip #5: Capitalize on Teachable Moments

Were you ever the unwilling recipient of a parent's lectures about life? If so, you have experienced firsthand how ineffective this teaching method can be. While it may be tempting to sit your children down and give a sermon about personal finance or family values, fight the urge. Instead, capitalize on teachable moments, those impromptu opportunities for learning that come up during the course of a day. If you are grocery shopping and your son is haphazardly throwing pre-packaged food into the cart, let him know you value locally grown products. Then discuss why you are willing to spend a bit more for these items as a way of expressing this belief. Teachable moments happen everywhere, from the movie theatre, to the mall, to the car ride home. Keep your eyes and ears open and use the moments as they arise.

While teachable moments often arise unplanned, it is a good idea to think about how your daily activities can be easily turned into opportunities for learning. For example, a ride to school can trigger a conversation about the money messages in your teen's favorite pop music. A trip to the grocery store is a great place to teach young people about reading price labels, comparison-shopping, and making a budget. Or the next time you watch a television show as a family, challenge your children to a contest to see who can discover the most money messages in the plot.

Teachable moments are everywhere. Just keep your eyes open and seize the opportunities when they appear.

Tip #6: Use Cash to Make the Lessons Real

Adam Carroll, financial educator and author of *Winning the Money Game*, decided to conduct an experiment with his children to test the theory that cash has a different effect on behavior than other forms of payment such as credit or debit cards, Apple Pay or online payments. One weekend, he and his children played the board game Monopoly using real money. Carroll discovered that his children were more conservative in their spending and savings when handling actual 20-, 50-, and 100-dollar bills than they were when using fake Monopoly money.

This experiment points to the importance of having your kids engage in cash transactions. They need to experience the pain of parting with money when they spend, which they don't feel with other forms of payment. Consider paying their allowance in cash and creating opportunities for them to save and spend using actual dollars and cents.

Tip #7: Encourage Money Talk between Siblings

When I speak to audiences about money, I ask attendees to raise their hands if they know their siblings' salary. Most people's hands remain by their sides. I then ask if they know how much their siblings paid for their houses. A few hands pop up, but not many. You see, money silence doesn't just impact parent–child relationships; it also affects the dynamic between brothers and sisters. This makes sense, because if you did not discuss money as a family, then your brother or sister may not feel like they have permission to ask about your financial life.

Encourage your kids to talk with their siblings about money. Not only can they serve as each other's sounding board when it comes to negotiating a salary, buying or selling a house, or making a large purchase, it can help when they are older and need to communicate about expenses related to eldercare or funeral arrangements. That is not a cheery thought, but it is based in reality. When parents get older, many siblings fight when they are suddenly put in the position of making financial decisions together. But if they have learned how to do so when they were younger, conflicts are less likely to occur when the time comes for your kids to take care of you.

In the next chapter, you will learn more about discussing money matters with parents as they age, and how having good money communication with your siblings can help.

Tip #8: Show, Don't Tell

We all know that actions speak louder than words. This is also true when it comes to your financial habits. Remember you are a powerful role model for your children, and often nonverbal communication sends a stronger message than words. It is imperative that your actions are consistent with the values you are trying to impart. For example, if you are teaching your children about caring for others, don't just write a check to your favorite charity. Instead, volunteer alongside of them and let them experience the sense of joy that comes with thoughtful, involved giving.

Tyler is a great example of a parent who desperately wants to do the right thing by his kids, but fails to practice what he preaches. Tyler works in sales and loves to spend his bonus on shiny new objects, but he lectures his two teenage boys about the value of saving and encourages them to create and live on a budget. "I just don't want them to have the financial problems I did in college." The problem is that Tyler's words don't match his behavior. What his sons see is their father impulsively spending. They don't see him saving, or living on a budget as he suggests they do. Until Tyler can show them through his financial habits the value of saving, his boys are likely to follow in their dad's footsteps and spend impulsively.

Tip #9: Let Failure Happen

It can be painful to watch, but kids need to experience failure firsthand. It helps them develop a sense of mastery when they must figure out how to correct the error and move on. Too often, parents with good intentions bail their children out of tough situations. Parent allow children to live rent-free, pay off their excessive credit card balance in full, or cover the legal bill that resulted from a child's bad behavior. When parents do this, young people don't learn how to be self-reliant. Instead, they start to believe they can't be self-sufficient and need mom and dad to rescue them.

Kaitlin is a perfect example of a young woman who never experienced failure. By the time I met with her, she had developed an eating disorder and was drinking heavily. Her mother was an accomplished lawyer and her father was a high-level business executive. Kaitlin had been sent away to a private high school and given everything she wanted. Her illness was the only thing that seemed to get the three of them in a room together.

After seeing Kaitlin for a few weeks, it became apparent to me that her eating disorder and drinking were cries for help. She wanted her parents to see her pain, but unfortunately, didn't know how to use her words to communicate with them. Instead, she starved herself until they noticed. The parents, well-intended but misguided, thought providing Kaitlin with expensive things, including the best mental health treatment available, would be the answer to her problems. By the time I started to work with her, it was clear that she didn't want to be rescued. What she really needed was to fail, and then learn how to brush herself off and get back up again.

I coached the parents to set some limits with Kaitlin, including financial ones. The first thing I recommended was that she get a part-time job and pay for a portion of her treatment. The idea was that earning money and then using it to pay for her sessions would help her understand how much her eating disorder was costing her and her family. It also would put her in a position to be part of the solution. Of course, the family fought the idea in the beginning, but eventually agreed to give it a try.

It turned out that Kaitlin enjoyed working and found that it gave her a sense of meaning. She started taking responsibility for the copay for each of her sessions. At first, she was resentful when she handed me the 20-dollar bill. But over time, something changed. Kaitlin started to enjoy contributing to her care. She even saved up to buy herself the Jimmy Choo shoes she wanted. "In the past, I just charged anything I wanted to my dad's Amex card. I would order a pair of new shoes a week. But these shoes are different—they are mine," she said, smiling.

Like most young women with eating disorders, Kaitlin took some time to recover. An important step for Kaitlin was finding out that she could rely on herself to pick up the pieces, and that her mom and dad would still love her if she started to take care of herself.

Let your kids fail, support them as they try to figure out how to correct the situation, but don't fix it for them. They may kick and scream in the short run, but will be forever grateful in adulthood.

Tip #10: Have Fun!

How many adults equate managing money with the words boring, dull, and dry? Too many! Learning about money and talking about it can be fun. So get creative and figure out entertaining activities to do with your children. Here are a few websites that will get your creative juices flowing.

Feed the Pig (http://www.feedthepig.org), created and maintained by the American Institute of CPAs, is a website that encourages users to put more money in their piggy banks. Sign up for savings reminders and use the resource material with your kids. It may just be worth a visit to the website to check out the Pig Mascot. If nothing else, it will make your children laugh.

SALT Money (http://www.saltmoney.org) is designed for college students ages 18 to 26, and is funded by American Student Assistance, a nonprofit that helps young people with student debt. Using motion graphics and gamification, this website is both entertaining and informative. Visit with your kids. Sign-up is required to access the full site.

Sammy the Rabbit (http://www.sammyrabbit.com) is aimed at children in first through third grade, and is full of free resources. Founder Sam X Renick, mentioned earlier in the chapter, is passionate about teaching kids how to be financially responsible and have fun in the process. Watch videos, listen to songs, or read stories together, all of them based on the idea that saving is a good habit.

Now that you know the 10 tips for teaching financial literacy, let's briefly discuss what parents who are affluent also need to consider.

Are We Rich? Special Considerations for Affluent Parents

Raising children to be financially savvy presents a unique challenge to affluent parents. How do you let your children enjoy a lifestyle that is rich in opportunity due to your success without spoiling them? For example, Sting, the musician worth an estimated $300 million, made the decision not to leave his six children an inheritance. He told reporters he wants his children to earn their own money and learn the value of hard work as he did growing up in a working-class family. Warren Buffet and Bill Gates have publicly echoed similar sentiments.

All parents want to rear healthy, self-sufficient children. When you have wealth, the question of how to do this is complicated. Some well-intended affluent parents go to extremes and don't talk openly about money with their children. The fear is if the next generation knows about the money they will become entitled, unmotivated, and overly dependent adults. While this concern is valid, the best way to protect your children from this fate is to engage in more communication, not less.

Clearly communicating your values to them and how you use wealth to express these ideals is paramount. Be explicit about what is important to you and why. For example, if you take your family to Europe every year because you want your children to benefit from learning about the world firsthand, tell them. Without an explanation about why you invested money in this trip, miscommunication can happen. Your intended message may be "education is important," but they walk away thinking "room service is awesome." Be sure to overtly communicate your family values and how you use your wealth to live by them.

Another area that is vital to raising financially savvy affluent children is helping them find their life purpose. This is an important stage of development for all young adults that can become more complicated if you are brought up in an affluent environment. While your teenager may not need to work, there is no substitute for the real-life experience of working at minimum wage and seeing the time, energy, and effort that goes into earning a living. A job also gives young people a sense of satisfaction and a feeling of accomplishment. It helps them decide what they enjoy doing, what they are good at, and how to get along with coworkers. These are all skills that will help them thrive in adulthood.

In the book *Raised Healthy, Wealthy & Wise*, author Coventry Edward-Pitts interviews 24 inheritors who she considered successful, defined as having a demonstrated ability to earn their own money, motivation to achieve personal goals, a strong sense of their identity, and the resilience to overcome setbacks in life. Edward-Pitt discovered that working was a key ingredient in raising financially intelligent heirs. It helped these young people develop the skills and knowledge to manage money and also gave meaning to their lives. While some of the interviewees admitted to complaining to their parents during their teens and early 20s about having to get a job, in the end they thanked them.

Raising healthy affluent children is a topic that several authors have covered, and is a field that continues to grow and evolve. If this is your family situation, reach out to your advisor for reading recommendations and help in talking to the next generation about wealth.

It's a Journey

Whether you are from an affluent home or one of modest means, raising financially intelligent children is a journey, not a one-time event. There will be many twists and turns along the way and many conversations. Be persistent in your commitment to break money silence with your children. Get support and education when you need it. Enlist family members to help you teach your next generation how to be financially savvy. And in the end, your children and their children will be thankful, because financial intelligence is truly a gift that every parent should try to give.

Summary

In this chapter, you learned about the challenges and rewards of raising financially intelligent kids. Whether you are a parent, older sibling, aunt, uncle, cousin, or family friend, remember these important facts.

- Parents are influential financial role models for the next generation and it's never too early or too late to engage your family in money talk.
- If you are reluctant to discuss money matters with your kids, you are not alone, but you need to fight the urge to give in to money silence.

- Discuss how you make financial decisions, and share your family values with your children as this gives context to the financial habits they see you engaging in.

- Capitalize on teachable moments, be creative, and have fun teaching the next generation how to be financially savvy.

- You don't have to have it all figured out to empower your kids to succeed financially. You simply must be willing to try.

Money Talk Challenge: Identifying Your Money Mentor Strengths

An important first step toward empowering the next generation to be financially intelligent is to identify your strengths as a money mentor. Below is an exercise I use with my graduate students to assess their knowledge and skills in ten areas. Despite these students being finance and accounting majors, they usually identify at least one or two areas where they need improvement. Don't be surprised if you have similar results.

Instructions

Step 1: Review the ten money skills detailed in Table 8.1, Assessing Your Financial Intelligence Strengths.[21]

Step 2: Put a check mark in the column titled "Mastery" or "Needs Improvement" based on your proficiency in this area of personal finance. *Mastery* means that you are knowledgeable and you practice this financial habit in your life. *Needs improvement* indicates that this is a financial topic that you need to learn more about before you feel capable of teaching this skill to others and/or you don't practice this skill in your life.

Step 3: Now add up the number of checks in each column. If you have achieved mastery in all areas, congratulations! Go out and mentor as many family members and friends as you can. Based on your current strengths, consider how you can be most beneficial to your children or the other young people in your life. For example, if you are great at tracking your money and spending wisely, then teach a young person this skill. If you are entrepreneurial, then coach a teen to start a lawn mowing service as a way to develop their business money management skills. What is the one action you will take to teach the next generation?

Step 4: If you are like most people and have a few checks in the "needs improvement" column, don't fret. It just means that you need to brush up on some aspects of your relationship with money. For each money skill you checked as "needs improvement," consider how to acquire more knowledge about this facet of finance or how to practice using this skill more often. Come up

Table 8.1   Assessing Your Financial Intelligence Strengths

Money Skills	Mastery	Needs Improvement
How to save		
How to keep track of money		
How to get paid what you are worth		
How to spend wisely		
How to talk about money		
How to live on a budget		
How to invest		
How to exercise the entrepreneurial spirit (business smarts)		
How to use credit		
How to use money to change the world (philanthropy)		

with one action you will take this week to improve your financial intelligence.

Here are a few ideas on how to increase your financial intelligence.

Ask a Friend or Family Member to Coach You

Is there someone in your family or your social circle who is good with money or investments? Consider asking this person to coach you on financial topics you want to learn more about. Usually people who enjoy finance are honored to be asked to teach others what they know. Not only is this an act of breaking money silence, it is a great way to learn more about money so you can fill your financial literacy gaps.

Start a Financially Focused Book Group

Book groups are a great way to learn more about money. Ask a few friends to join you, then together select one financially themed book to read each month. Include books that run the gamut from personal finance to money psychology to the stock market. Consider books like the *Big Short* (about the corruption on Wall Street that led to the Great Recession), *On Your Own Two Feet* (about managing finances when you are 20-something), or *The Financial Wisdom of Ebenezer Scrooge* (about money mindsets). Host a potluck dinner and spend the evening discussing the book and learning more about finance.

Work with an Advisor

Financial advisors make great teachers. If you are currently working with an advisor, ask if he would be willing to teach you more about finances. Also, inquire about how he can help you teach the next generation about finances. If you are not currently working with an advisor, consider contacting one to find out the type of education they offer. Many advisors offer seminars or teach at local schools as part of their business development activities. Take advantage of these offerings. If an advisor comes on too strong with a sales pitch, try another one. There are many wonderful professionals who are more interested in a long-term relationship than a quick sale. Of course, you will need to compensate them for their time, but this is often a worthwhile investment.

For Advisors

Use the "Identifying Your Money Mentor Strengths" activity with your clients to assess their basic financial knowledge and skill set. Based on their answers, develop an education plan to help them close their knowledge and skill gaps. Encourage them to use their strengths to teach the next generation about money. Depending on the ages of their children, invite the entire family to join you to discuss creative and fun ways to talk about money together. Use this as an opportunity to meet the next generation, or at least plant the seed in your clients' mind that facilitating money talk is a service you provide.

To help you take action, list three clients you will share this coaching activity with in the next 90 days.

CHAPTER NINE

Raising Financially Fit Parents

It's paradoxical that the idea of living a long life appeals to everyone, but the idea of getting old doesn't appeal to anyone.
—Andy Rooney, American radio and television writer

When I was in my twenties, I joked with my mom and dad that raising parents was hard work. I really didn't know how challenging it would be until years later when they started aging. All of a sudden, I needed to act more like a parent than a child. My mother had dementia and my father was her primary caregiver. I would "babysit" my mom so my dad could play golf. I would go to medical appointments, take notes, and oversee the healthcare and insurance paperwork. Once invincible in my eyes, my father regularly turned to me for emotional support. Yes, parenting my elderly mom and dad was indeed hard work.

There are societal norms for how parents should act when raising their children. But there are no such guidelines for an adult child taking care of an elderly parent. It feels like your roles have been reversed. Once the child, you are now the caregiver. But the person you are taking care of is still your parent. It's confusing, stressful, and at times wonderful.

Now add money to the mix. When, what, and how do you assist your elderly parents with their finances? Do you dare to break money silence and ask them questions about their estate plan, healthcare coverage, and end-of-life directives? Or do you remain mute and hope for the best? If you have brothers or sisters, do you include them in the conversation, and if so, when? Will your mom and dad be receptive to your assistance or upset that you are nosing around in their business? The list of questions goes on and on, and there are no easy answers.

Given the money silence that runs rampant in our society and tends to be more pronounced in older generations, engaging your parents in money talk is both taxing and necessary. Just look at the statistics.

- Seven in ten adults find it difficult to talk to their families about who will make financial decisions for an aging parent or relative.[1]
- Fifty-four percent of adult children would rather have the sex talk with their kids than the aging talk with their mom and dad.[2]
- Over half of adult children have not discussed senior care issues, including finances, with their aging parents.[3]
- By 2050, the number of people 65 years and older with Alzheimer's disease is projected to triple from 5 million to 13.8 million.[4]
- Currently, the average lifetime cost of care for a patient with Alzheimer's disease is $174,000, and by 2050 the out-of-pocket care expenses for a family are estimated to rise by more than 400%.[5]

Given the increase in longevity due to medical advances, caring for an aging parent is likely to be in your future or your partner's. It may be anxiety-provoking to approach your parents (or your adult children) about this topic, but it can save you heartache in the long run.

Zachary's mother knows this firsthand. "Unfortunately, before my grandpa passed away, he and my mom never discussed money. When he died, my parents were overwhelmed. My mom didn't know if there were enough savings to pay for the funeral, whether her father had outstanding bills, or how much of an inheritance she would receive." Zachary's mom eventually figured it out, but found that worrying about these financial matters made her grieving process more complicated and stressful. She made a promise to Zachary that she would discuss finances with him so he would not be left with the same burden.[6]

Approaching your parents to discuss money matters can be daunting, but these conversations are necessary. I was fortunate to have a father who took the initiative to have a money talk with my sister and me when my mother became ill. But I know that I am the exception to the rule. Many of my friends, colleagues, and clients have shared stories about wanting to speak up but being initially fearful to do so. In the end, those who broke money silence with their families discovered there was a silver lining to having these dialogues. Many learned things about their parents they never knew, and others came to really appreciate the sacrifices their parents made to give them a secure and happy childhood. In the end, all were satisfied that they tried to discuss money with their parents and that they took steps to provide the next generation with a roadmap on how to do this.

In this chapter, you will hear stories from adult children who have broken money silence with their aging parents. You will learn strategies for starting these conversations, and techniques for keeping the dialogue going. In addition, you will learn how to cope with a resistant parent, how to collaborate with your siblings, and when to reach out for professional help. If you are a mature parent, I will also shed some light on how you can be proactive in sharing your financial information with your adult children.

Mom and Dad, We Need to Talk

Something happens to make you realize that things are changing. Your mom starts repeating herself. Your father keeps losing his keys. One of your parents needs emergency surgery. It hits you: "My parents aren't young anymore."

Due to medical advances, people are living longer than ever before. The upside is that many senior citizens enjoy active lives, continue to work, and remain productive members of our society. The downside is that the chance of you having to care for an elderly parent at some point in your adulthood has increased. Even if your mom and dad don't develop dementia, 50% of seniors 85 years and older suffer from some type of cognitive impairment.[7] It is highly likely that at some point your mom and dad won't be as able to manage their financial lives as they did when you were growing up. The best way to handle this reality is to engage your parents in a money talk. Of course, the tricky part is getting them to agree to participate.

Financial conversations with parents can be delicate and challenging. Often, older generations have money mindsets that reinforce the notion that money silence "protects" them. Siblings have different opinions about when and how to engage in this conversation. And if you are a parent yourself, you may find it challenging to carve out time in your busy schedule to prepare for and engage in this discussion.

Tricky or not, money talk with aging parents protects the entire family. It helps your parents plan for their needs as they age and gives them a chance to spend their remaining years according to their wishes. It helps you understand the types of financial and emotional demands in your own future.

As someone who has participated in quite a few money talks with my parents, I can assure you that it is worth your time and energy. As in most families, there were some disagreements and misunderstandings. But when it came time to say goodbye to my mother, I knew that we had done the best we could to support her during her final years.

My hope is that you too will benefit from money dialogues with your parents. One thing is for sure—you will never know unless you ask.

You Never Know Until You Ask

Anticipating a financial conversation with a parent can be anxiety-producing. This discomfort can ignite a series of "what-if" questions, such as:

- "What if I ask about his finances and my dad thinks I am being greedy and ungrateful?"
- "What if I tell my mom I am concerned about her ability to make ends meet, and she sees me as a rude and opinionated brat?"
- "What if I have a money talk with my parents and they feel badgered by my questions?"

The problem with "what-if" questions is they raise anxiety, instead of quelling it. The underlying rationale for these inquires is well-intended. By playing out different "what-if" scenarios, you are attempting to control the uncontrollable. But alas, you can't predict the outcome of a conversation before you have it. In other words, you don't know how your parent or loved one will react, until you extend an invitation to engage in a financial conversation. You can continue to drive yourself crazy wondering what might be, or you can find out by daring to break money silence.

Juan, a 52-year-old divorcé, worried for months about asking his father if he had a will and who was named executor. After his divorce, Juan knew the value of having the proper legal documents in place. But he feared his father would think less of him for asking. To his surprise, his father was open to the conversation. As Juan put it, "When I asked my father who was the executor of the will, I worried he would see it as an attempt to take control of the family finances. Instead, he seemed relieved to finally have one of us discuss what was already on his mind."

Instead of spending time thinking about all the potential negative outcomes, consider the possibility that your parent may be receptive to a money talk. Remember that inviting elderly parents to this type of discussion is a caring gesture. With this mindset, let's review some tips that will increase the likelihood of a successful outcome.

Successfully Engaging Parents in Money Talks

As previously discussed, engaging in healthy financial dialogue requires thoughtful preparation, emotional intelligence, and good communication skills. Here are 10 tips to consider when discussing financial matters with an aging parent.

Tip #1: Identify and Process Your Feelings before the Invitation

Talking to parents about their estate plans, financial situation, and healthcare wishes is emotional business. Before you invite them to discuss these matters, take time to process your own feelings. You may be annoyed, angry, frustrated, sad, or scared about their situation. Whatever your emotional state, know that it is normal and healthy to have a reaction to your parents aging. Keep in mind that your feelings may change over time.

You are more likely to approach your parent in a calm, respectful manner if you first give yourself time and space to experience your feelings. Otherwise, your emotions may get in the way of having an adult discussion with your parent.

Sean is a perfect example. As his dad's memory began to fade, Sean became very sad. Every time he visited with his father, Sean tried to push down his sadness. His dad had taught him that crying was for girls. The problem was that every time Sean fought off his sorrow, he ended up irritated and frustrated with his father. "My dad would repeat himself a lot and tell the same stories. It just made me so angry that I would snap at him. It wasn't his fault, but I couldn't stop."

Eventually, Sean decided to work with a counselor. In these sessions, he realized that getting angry with his dad was a way of protecting himself from his intense grief. It also was his attempt to make his dad proud, as he never liked criers. Once Sean identified his feelings and had a safe place to talk about slowly losing his dad to Alzheimer's disease, his time with his father was more enjoyable. He just needed to process his feelings first.

Kelly's feelings were different than Sean's feelings, but just as valid. Her 69-year-old father ended up hospitalized and she discovered that her parents had no estate plan and had not financially prepared for their golden years. She explains, "At first, I was resentful. My thought was 'Mom and Dad, why didn't you financially plan for your future?' I feel like this was my parents' responsibility. They are the parents and I am the kid." Kelly realized that she needed to process these feelings before she approached her parents regarding the matter. Like many adult children, she felt burdened by her parents leaning on her for help at this stage of their lives. Married and raising two teenagers, Kelly has her own business and already felt spread too thin.[8]

"When you are younger, you think your parents just know it all. And then suddenly, you become an adult and you start raising your own family and that veil starts to disappear." Once Kelly came to grips with the fact that her parents were just people, faults and all, she could then reach out and offer her help. As she puts it, "The good news is this situation with my folks made me say, 'I don't want to do this to *my* kids!'"[9]

It is important to acknowledge, discuss, and process your own feelings before you approach your mom or dad. Do this with an understanding partner, trusted friend, or a counselor. By investing time in processing your own emotions, you will be better able to approach your parents in a calm, respectful manner. Breathing helps, too!

Tip #2: Extend a Loving Invitation

Lead with loving intentions and let your parents know that you want to discuss their financial life because you care. Begin by saying something like, "I know this might be difficult for you to talk about, but I care enough about you to want to make sure you're taken care of as you age. Can we find a time to discuss what plans you have made and how I might be able to help you in making sure everything is taken care of?" Or, if there has been a specific healthcare crisis, you may want to say, "These last few months have been hard on you as you recover from your heart attack. I noticed that paying bills and keeping up with finances has gotten a little more challenging. Can we find a time to talk about how I might be able to help you keep up with your bills so you can continue to focus on getting well?" This approach shows that you care and allows the other person to decide when and where to have the conversation.

Tip #3: Ask During a Quiet Time

Finding a quiet time to ask your parents to engage in a financial dialogue with you is essential. Be certain to avoid busy holiday times or events where you are likely to be distracted. While you may want to talk *today* about money, remember your parent may need some time to adjust to the idea of breaking their money silence with you.

"When I first asked my mother about her estate plan, she was at the dining room table. The entire family was there as we had just finished a holiday meal. The minute I said something I wanted to take it back," Sheri said. A week later, Sheri went to her mother's house for tea. It was just the two of them. She apologized for embarrassing her mother at the holiday table and explained why she was interested in the estate plan. When she told her mother that her good friend's mother died without a will and now the family was in court fighting over their inheritance, her mother forgave her and welcomed her questions. In Sheri's case, timing was everything.

When it comes to inviting a parent to share their financial information with you, especially if your family has a long-standing tradition of money silence, find a quiet time to do so. Communicate your loving intent, and then give your parent a chance to digest this request. This will set you and your loved one up for success when the actual conversation occurs.

Tip #4: Be Specific about Your Concerns

When sharing your concerns with a parent, be specific. For example, if you are worried that your mother has been the victim of a telephone scam targeted at the elderly, let her know that. Say something like, "Mom, I love you very much and I want what is best for you. Last month, I noticed a $100 charge on the credit card bill from the Orphans and Widow Fund. I did some research and I found out that this organization doesn't exist. I am worried that you may have been taken advantage of financially. I would like to help you not get hurt like this again in the future. What do you think?" If you express loving concern and are specific about the cause of your worry, your parent is more likely to understand your actions. In addition, asking for their input allows your parent to maintain dignity while accepting assistance.

For many adult children, their anxiety about having a money talk leads to rash actions. While the intent is to be helpful, the lack of specific data confuses a parent or makes them more defensive. For example, consider what might happen if you were concerned about the charge on the credit card but said, "Mom, you can't handle your finances any more, I need to take over." Chances are your mom would get angry and not accept your help. You'll increase the likelihood of cooperation by being specific.

Tip #5: Keep the Conversations Brief

Once your parent has agreed to a money talk, keep the conversation brief. You may have a million questions for your mom or dad, but asking one or two questions at a time is better than bombarding your parent with inquires. While you may have been thinking about this money talk for months leading up to it, this is a new conversation for your parent. Give them time to digest what you are saying and respond. It is better to have three 30-minute talks than one 90-minute conversation. Not only does this keep everyone focused on one task or discussion item at a time, it helps everyone stay calm and rational.

Phyllis made the mistake of engaging her father in a marathon money talk. He had finally agreed to share his financial data with her. She lived several hours away, so she drove up for a long weekend. Phyllis had a list of all the questions that she wanted to ask her dad, and a list of all the paperwork to collect. Naively, she thought she could gather all this information during her visit.

By noon the first day of her visit, her 80-year-old father looked exhausted. He seemed to be getting more confused and his answers started to contradict each other. While his memory was still intact, it was too much to expect of him at his age. She revealed, "I overdid it. My hope was to get it all done in one day, so we could enjoy the rest of our visit. After a few hours, I realized that my expectations were unrealistic. Now I visit him once every other week and we spend about thirty minutes a day on financial stuff. It is painfully slow for me but eventually we will get it done."

Depending on your personality, pacing yourself may be challenging. Remember that your parents may not be as quick as they once were and that taking it slow may make the most sense. Keep in mind that short money talks often yield better long-term results.

Tip #6: Give Your Parent Control Whenever Possible

A big part of aging is dealing with a loss of control over your physical and mental health. Elderly parents know that in time, they will need more support, but often don't want to face this reality. When discussing how you can help them with financial matters, reassure them that this is not an attempt to take over their life, simply an offer to help them as they age. Whenever possible, invite your parent to decide what to address and when. By doing so, you are demonstrating that you are there to support them, not to take over.

When my mother was first diagnosed with Alzheimer's disease, my priority was to find her the best doctors and treatment to prolong her memory for as long as possible. Conversely, my father wanted to solely focus on the legal issues. At first, I felt resistant to meet with attorneys. Then I realized that my dad, an engineer who thrives on data, found comfort in the structure of these appointments. He was losing his wife of 54 years, and becoming focused on the legal paperwork really helped him cope with the immense sadness of the situation. While finding the best doctors and protecting my parents' assets were both worthwhile goals, it was important that my dad felt in control. So I supported him in figuring out all the legalities, until he was ready to turn his attention to her medical care.

Parents are used to being in control, so giving them choices helps them maintain their dignity as they age. Even if it's difficult, ask your mom for her input and then really listen to her requests. Or give your dad a few options and then start with the one that is his priority. While you may want to proceed differently, know that these small gestures go a long way in reassuring your loved one that their voice still matters.

Tip #7: Take Baby Steps

When a parent needs help with their finances, there are often many pieces in the puzzle. Instead of tackling them all at once, it is important to take baby steps. Otherwise, you risk overwhelming your parent as well as yourself.

Kelly, mentioned earlier, found this a very useful strategy. "I offered to help break tasks down into small bits so my parents, especially my father, would not get overwhelmed. At first I asked, 'What different savings and checking accounts do you have and where are they?' A week would go by, and then I would go to my parents' house for Sunday dinner. Before I left, my dad gave me a piece of paper containing all the banking information I had requested."[10]

Taking action and checking things off your to-do list may make you feel good. But you need to consider how it might impact your loved one. Often as people age, their cognitive ability is impaired, making it wise to break complex processes into small, doable steps.

Tip #8: Be Curious

Remember that a healthy dose of curiosity can save a conversation. When approaching a parent, tap into your beginner's mind and wonder about their perspective. This can be challenging as you have a long history with a parent. Remember that when you have known someone for a long time, it becomes easier to fall into the trap of reading minds, or jumping to conclusions. Fight this urge and remember this is a new conversation at a new point in time in your relationship. Wonder, and leave your assumptions at the door.

Aaron grew frustrated with his 71-year-old mother when she refused to have knee replacement surgery. She walked with a limp and lived in pain every day. Every time he raised the issue of his mother getting surgery, she would change the subject. Aaron even offered to pay for the procedure but his mom refused. It was not until his wife, Alicia, asked her mother-in-law why she didn't want a knee replacement that the real reason for her resistance to surgery surfaced. His mother feared that she would lose her job if she took too much time off from work. It took Alicia's curiosity to uncover the reason that Aaron's mom declined surgery.

It is often what people *don't* talk about that is the most important. Getting curious and asking open-ended, probing questions will help you uncover this information. Let go of knowing why your parent won't do something, and instead invite them to tell you.

Tip #9: Abide by the Kingsbury Rules for Fighting Fair Financially

In Chapter 5, I shared the Kingsbury Rules of Fighting Fair Financially. These include practicing active listening, using "I" statements, and sometimes agreeing to disagree. Remember that money talk with your elderly parents can be emotional. Therefore, if the conversation gets overheated or a member of the family gets overly defensive, take a time-out. Set another meeting date in the near future that allows everyone to calm down and refocus on the task at hand. The most effective communication happens when all parties are open to hearing each other as opposed to fighting.

Every time Devin tried to approach her mother about moving to assisted living, her mother got angry and stopped talking to her. Devin's dad had died a few years ago and as the only child, she felt responsible for her mother's safety. "We just could not see eye to eye on the matter." Eventually, Devin took a friend's advice and told her mother that it was okay if they disagreed, but she was going to remain concerned about her mother's living situation. "That seemed to break the ice. The next week, my mom started asking questions about the assisted living place. Once she didn't have to agree with me, she seemed open to considering it. It seemed like if she could blame me, then getting more support was okay."

Money conversations can be challenging, but if you practice effective communication techniques, you will eventually reach a mutual understanding. It may not be the exact ending you anticipated, but usually it is a compromise that works for all involved.

Tip #10: Enlist a Trusted Advisor to Facilitate Difficult Conversations

Financial advisors are great resources when it comes to helping you talk to your parents about money, estate plans, and end-of-life wishes. Don't hesitate to use your advisor as a resource for information, support, or guidance on this matter. Acting as a neutral party, the advisor can offer their financial expertise, facilitate a difficult conversation, and provide referrals to other professionals such as estate planning attorneys, healthcare advocates, home health aides, assisted living facilities, and nursing homes.

Joe Norris, CFP®, watched his 95-year-old mother struggle with dementia for 13 years before she died. He described his experience with her illness as watching his mother go down a flight of stairs very slowly. "Each time she went down the next set of stairs, I knew she would never climb back up." Joe's personal experience has made him very passionate about helping his clients and their families as they age.[11]

Joe sees his role as a financial advisor as being an advocate for his client, but also as someone who can alert the rest of the family when his client seems to need more help. Some of his elderly clients are resistant to including their children in the financial planning process, but persistence pays off. Joe finds that over time, his aging clients often agree to involve their adult children in some capacity.[12]

If you are a mature parent, you can also work with an advisor to facilitate conversations with your adult children. By enlisting the help of a professional, you are breaking money silence in your family and also giving your adult children a roadmap for how to engage in money talk with their own children. At the end of this chapter, I discuss some things to consider if you decide to be proactive and invite your adult children to have a legacy conversation.

Talking about More Than Money

As with most financial conversations, talking with parents involves money and a host of other things. As mentioned in Chapter 7, these are often referred to as legacy conversations. These money talks help you understand the values your parents want to pass on to you and the next generation, as well as how they want to be cared for as they age. If you start with your parents' values in mind, it can help the conversation get off on the right foot.

For example, if you ask your mom how much is in her savings account, she might get defensive. But if you inquire about her money mindset about saving money, she may be excited to share her philosophy. Yes, you eventually need to get into the numbers (see Sidebar 9.1, Ten Financial Questions to Ask Aging Parents), but first try to put yourself into your parents' shoes and discover what makes your parents tick.

Start by asking your parents what it feels like to break money silence with you. This question opens the door for your parents to discuss the emotions related to discussing finances with you, or other people. Explore their money history and what they learned about money growing up. If your parents seem interested, tell them about what you learned in this book about money mindsets and how thoughts and feelings impact financial habits. Share with your parents one thing they taught you about money that has been very helpful, and ask them to share a story about what they learned from their parents. By sharing something positive, you are demonstrating to your parents that a money talk can be pleasant, and even enjoyable.

Remember that most people, even your parents, have mixed feelings about money and wealth. By asking your parents to share their thoughts about money and letting them know a valuable lesson you learned as a child, you are modeling what a healthy money talk looks like.

Of course, if your parent is more data-driven and would prefer to get right into the facts and figures, then do so. Use the questions in the sidebar to guide the conversation. Like all money conversations, it is best to meet the other person where they feel most comfortable.

SIDEBAR 9.1 TEN FINANCIAL QUESTIONS TO ASK AGING PARENTS

1. Have you named a durable power of attorney that allows someone else to manage your finances if you are unable to do so? If so, who, and how can I contact them?

2. Where do you keep your financial records and corresponding user names and passcodes?

3. What are your bank account numbers and names of your financial institutions?

4. What are your monthly expenses and how do you pay the bills currently (online, automatic payment, check, other)?

5. How much is your annual income and where does it come from?

6. Does your monthly income cover your monthly expenses?

7. Do you receive Medicare, Medicaid, or Social Security?

8. What type of medical health insurance do you have? Where is your medical health insurance card kept, and how might I be able to get your insurance policy number in case of an emergency?

9. Do you have long-term care insurance, disability insurance, and/or life insurance? If so, where are the policies kept and can I have access to them?

10. Do you have a financial advisor or accountant? If so, can I attend a meeting with you or can you sign a release so I can talk with this professional?

Adapted from Sollitto, Marlo. 2014. "10 Things You Should Know About Your Parent's Finances." *Amac.* December 16. Accessed January 26, 2017. https://amac.us/10-things-know-parents-finances/.

When Your Request Falls on Deaf Ears

In Chapter 5, I discussed how it takes two willing participants to have a productive money talk. The same is true when you are trying to engage an aging parent in a financial dialogue. In some instances, time and persistence pays off. In other situations, only a financial or health crisis brings the other person around.

Just as you can break through a romantic partner's resistance to discussing money, you can also do so with a parent. You can use the broken record technique, for example. This is the strategy where you make multiple requests before the other person agrees to participate in the dialogue. For example, if your parent insists he does not need help, say something like, "I understand why you don't want my help now. Can I check back in with you in two weeks and see how things are going?" Then in two weeks, follow up. Like a broken record, you just keep checking in and waiting until your parent agrees to receive your support. This approach respects your parent's perspective but keeps the lines of communication open. Often a parent's pride may make it challenging for them to show any weaknesses to their offspring. If you are a parent yourself, you may be able to identify and empathize with this struggle.

Another idea is to capitalize on teachable moments, just as you might with a son or daughter when you are teaching them how to be financially intelligent. For example, if you are at your mother's house and she complains about a late fee on her utility bill, use this as an opening to gently inquire about the late fee and the reason the payment was past due. Be careful not to turn this into an "I told you so" moment. Remember, you are just trying to gather information to help persuade your mom that she may benefit from some support. But let her keep her dignity in the process. Your parent could just be fearful of the aging process and under the false impression that if you don't admit that your memory is failing, it won't actually happen.

Consider the fact that you may be forced to wait to have a money talk until a crisis occurs. A crisis often turns an optional money conversation into a mandatory one. While discussing finances during a crisis is not ideal, for some parents this is the only time they will agree to share their financial lives with their adult children. Remember that your parents are from an older generation that may have been discouraged from openly expressing their thoughts and feelings with their children.

If your loved one is stubborn and refuses to talk, expect to have feelings about it. Often these emotions are strong as they tap into early childhood wounds. Find a safe place to process these feelings. Lean on a trusted friend or partner, work with a counselor, or talk about your concerns with your advisor. Often what shifts a long-standing family dynamic is someone in the family doing something different. This produces a ripple effect, like a pebble thrown into a still pond. Communication patterns slowly shift as the ripples reverberate outward.

Moving from Sibling Rivalry to Collaboration

The beauty of a family is that it is made up of several generations of individuals with diverse personalities and viewpoints. While you share a history together, it is unrealistic to think you and your siblings will agree on every decision when it comes to caring for an elderly parent or impaired family member. Expect and respect differences. Don't waste time trying to convince others to agree with you. Instead, focus on trying to understand each other.

When you are talking to your siblings about an elderly parent, remember what you learned in Chapter 6 about curiosity. Use curious questions to discover their impression of your parents' financial needs. Tap into your beginner's mind and wonder out loud about their viewpoint on when and how to step in and support your mom or dad. Remember that every child has a different relationship with a parent, and you can use these dynamics to your advantage.

Muriel, the oldest of five adult children, is a great example of how family dynamics contribute to some problems but also can be the source of some solutions. For months, she had tried to get her mother to stop driving, as she was concerned about her safety and the safety of others. Her siblings didn't live close by and thought Muriel was overreacting. Muriel and her mother had a turbulent relationship since high school so her siblings expected them to fight.

Eventually, Muriel called her brother Rafael to help out. He was the baby of the family and in Muriel's eyes, their mom's favorite. Rafael was reluctant to talk to his mother about her driving. But Muriel knew that if he asked their mom to stop, she would. Mom always listened to him. Eventually, Rafael agreed to give it a try, as he could see how worried Muriel was becoming.

The following week, Rafael visited his mother and asked her to stop driving temporarily. He said, "Let me hold on to your car keys for a while. You can see what it is like to not drive and if you really are unhappy we can talk about it again." Mom agreed and never asked for the keys back. At first, Muriel was frustrated. Her numerous requests for her mom to stop driving had fallen on deaf ears so many times. But then she felt relieved because her mom was safe. This experience taught her that going forward she would decide how to best use the family dynamics to support her parent.

But what happens if you are worried about your parents because you think one of your siblings is taking advantage of them? Maybe you have a sister who, despite being in her mid-fifties, still expects your parents to pay for her and her children's expenses. Or you have a brother in his mid-forties who always seems to be between jobs. He's labeled the black sheep of the family, but your mother takes pity on him, slipping him money every time he comes around the house. Do you stay quiet or do you speak up?

My friend Niki faced this dilemma recently. She is married with four children and doing well financially. Conversely, her younger brother Jon has a history of troubled relationships and financial misfortune. When Jon separated from his wife and moved into their mom's apartment, Niki became concerned about her mother's financial situation. She explained, "My mum lives on a fixed government income and is paying for my brother's food, his rent, and giving him spending money like when we were kids. She sees Jon as her little boy, but he is a grown man and can certainly buy his own groceries."[13]

As the months passed, Niki became more frustrated with her brother's financial dependence on their mother. It was keeping her up at night and she knew she had to address the issues. To Niki's surprise, Jon showed up one day at her house and took her and the kids sailing and to dinner. "After he offered to pay for our meal, I asked Jon how his pending divorce might impact his finances. His answer revealed that he had no clue that Mum might be financially stretched now that he was living with her. When I raised this concern with him, we ended up having a wonderful conversation."[14]

Niki's tendency was to lecture her brother and tell him what to do, based on her own money mindset and impression of the situation. By changing her tactics and becoming more curious about her brother's intentions, she not only emotionally felt better, but her mother's financial situation improved. She recently found out that Jon had started paying rent and was giving her mother a few hundred dollars a month toward the food bill.

Conversations between siblings can get complicated. Past family dynamics come into play and old wounds can be reignited. This is why breaking money silence and having a money talk is so important. Check your assumptions at the door, and be open to learning more about the other person's viewpoint. In the end, you may still disagree, but at least you have more perspective and can pride yourselves on acting like two adults.

When to Ask for Help

There are certain times when no matter what technique you employ or which angle you approach it from, your parents or loved ones are not able to have a productive conversation about money. If this happens, it is a sign that you may need to ask for help. I realize that this can be complicated, as it requires you to break through another layer of money silence. But reaching out and enlisting support from a trained, neutral party is a prudent decision. I have seen many families overcome communication roadblocks simply by hiring someone to facilitate money conversations and hold the members of the family accountable for their actions.

Here are some telltale signs that it may be time to reach out for support.

You Are Getting Nowhere Fast

You feel like you are in the movie *Groundhog Day*, where the characters wake up every day to find it is February 2 and the day's events unfold exactly the same way each time. If you have tried to discuss money matters with your elderly parents, but the conversation is just not progressing, or it feels like you are having the same talk again and again, it is time to ask for help.

You Are Emotionally Drained

You are tired and exhausted from caring for an elderly parent. You may have been able to have an initial money conversation, but the stress you are experiencing is high. You often feel depressed, anxious, or angry, and you need a place to express these emotions. This is a good time to reach out to a licensed counselor who is trained in family dynamics and comprehends the emotional toll of being an adult child in your situation. It is not uncommon for adult children to enter short-term counseling during this life transition.

You Need Financial Expertise

Healthcare and eldercare options are complex, and it helps to have an advisor who can help you sort through your financial options. If you currently work with an advisor, set up an appointment to discuss your needs. Your family situation has an impact on your financial planning; therefore, it makes sense to fill your advisor in. If you don't currently work with an advisor, this may be a good reason to hire one. Advisors can help you and your parents narrow down the options, and evaluate the monetary impact of each scenario. Many advisors work as a member of a team, so they can also refer you to attorneys, healthcare advocates, insurance agents, and other related professionals as part of your client engagement.

Your Family Just Can't Get Along

Every family has its own communication style, and some styles are better equipped for working through difficult times such as caring for an elderly parent. If you find that you and your family members are constantly fighting, it is time to reach out and learn new communication skills. A licensed counselor or family wealth consultant can provide this type of communication skills training. If your family doesn't want to participate with you, it is okay to start the process alone.

Your Parent Is Unsafe

It is important that your elderly parent is physically and emotionally safe. If you feel as if your parent is not, then it is time to reach out to your parent's doctor, or call Adult Protective Services in your area. (See the Resource Guide for more information about this agency.) If you are concerned, it is better to act on the side of caution and reach out and let a professional trained in working with the elderly assess your situation. The worst thing that can happen is that you are wrong, and you demonstrate how much you love your mom or dad.

Table 9.1 lists professionals and a brief description of their services. This list is not exhaustive, but it should give you an idea of where to start when you are looking for assistance.

Liz is a great example of how reaching out for support can move the conversation forward. As the adult daughter of a retired police officer, Liz was frustrated when her father repeatedly refused to talk to her about his estate plan. Finally, Liz decided to get support and she contacted an estate attorney for a consultation.

Liz attended the first meeting alone and discussed her concerns regarding her father. The attorney coached Liz on how to approach her father again, and also validated that while her situation was frustrating, it was not uncommon. A week later, Liz asked her dad to meet with the attorney to discuss his options and reiterated that there was no obligation to take

Table 9.1 What Type of Support Do You Need?

Professional Type	Services Provided
Eldercare Coach	Emotional support, referrals to care facilitators and providers, and action-oriented coaching
Elder Law Attorney	Legal documents and guidance related to eldercare and estate planning
Family Wealth Consultant	Family communication training, money talk facilitation, collaboration with financial advisors
Financial Advisor	Financial planning, healthcare cost analysis, insurance information, and money talk facilitation
Licensed Counselor	Stress management, supportive therapy, family communication training, conflict resolution

any action. To her surprise, her father agreed. "Having the estate attorney in the room with Dad and me changed the tone of the conversation. It also changed the outcome. In forty-five minutes, I learned more about my dad than I had in forty-five years. He still hasn't agreed to draft a will, but I think he is getting closer."

Professionals like counselors, attorneys, and advisors are available and happy to assist you in this process. They offer expertise, and an objective view of your family's situation. Don't waste your time being stuck; get help and find out how to move the conversation forward.

Breaking money silence with your parents as they age is necessary if you want to financially and emotionally protect them. As an adult child, you may be the first one in your family to try to create a roadmap for these conversations. By following the advice in this chapter and enlisting support for yourself during this process, you will have done your best to raise a financially fit parent.

Summary

In this chapter, you learned tips and tools for breaking money silence with aging parents. Here are some things to remember.

- It is common for parents to want to maintain control as they age. Respect this desire by approaching them with loving intent, at a quiet time, and in a manner that lets your parent maintain dignity.
- Process your feelings about a parent's inevitable physical and mental decline before approaching them to talk about money.

- Use your family's dynamics to your advantage and carefully consider who is the best person to approach your parent when making a request.

- Know that some parents, especially those from the traditional generation, may refuse to talk about their finances with you. All you can do is try to open the lines of communication.

- Caring for an elderly parent is emotionally taxing. Ask for support from trusted friends, family members, a counselor, or an advisor when needed.

Money Talk Challenge: Preparing for a Money Talk with an Aging Parent

Careful and thoughtful preparation for a money talk with an aging parent often is the key to a good outcome. Find some quiet time to consider the behavioral, emotional, financial, and physical signs that warrant your concern and desire to help. Below are some examples of each indicator and a place for you to write down your specific observations. Be careful not to rush to judgment or diagnose your parent. Some of these signs are part of the natural aging process, and only medical doctors can diagnose a particular illness or dementia. Use these signs as a checklist to organize your thoughts so you can express your desire to help.

- *Behavioral Indicators.* Examples of behavioral signs of aging include unopened mail, cluttered home, rotten food in the refrigerator, decrease in bathing and cleanliness, decrease in social activities, and loss of interest in a hobby.

    1. What specific behavioral indicators do you observe?
    2. Using an "I" statement, how might you gently communicate what you observe and why it concerns you?
    3. Ideally, what action would you like your parent to take?
    4. How might you assist your parent in taking this action?
    5. Who else might be of service to you in addressing this issue?

- *Emotional Indicators.* Examples of emotional signs of aging include increased confusion, forgetfulness, anxiety, depression, irritability, or mood swings.

    1. What specific emotional indicators do you observe?
    2. Using an "I" statement, how might you gently communicate what you observe and why it concerns you?
    3. Ideally, what action would you like your parent to take?
    4. How might you assist your parent in taking this action?
    5. Who else might be of service to you in addressing this issue?

- *Financial Indicators.* Examples include missing payments, bounced checks, losing track of bills, late fees, donations to unknown solicitors, and inability to perform financial tasks that were easily completed in the past.

  1. What specific financial indicators do you observe?
  2. Using an "I" statement, how might you gently communicate what you observe and why it concerns you?
  3. Ideally, what action would you like your parent to take?
  4. How might you assist your parent in taking this action?
  5. Who else might be of service to you in addressing this issue?

- *Physical Indicators.* Examples include lack of mobility, health issues (such as heart disease, cancer, or other chronic illnesses), decreased eyesight, hearing loss, and difficulty verbally expressing wishes.

  1. What specific physical indicators do you observe?
  2. Using an "I" statement, how might you gently communicate what you observe and why it concerns you?
  3. Ideally, what action would you like your parent to take?
  4. How might you assist your parent in taking this action?
  5. Who else might be of service to you in addressing this issue?

  Example:

  - Observation: *I specifically noticed that my mother is losing her eyesight and has forgotten to pay several of her bills.*
  - "I" Statement: *"Mom, I love you very much and I notice that your eyesight has diminished over the last few months. I am wondering if this may be why some of your bills have gone unpaid? What do you think?"*
  - Action: *I would like her to automate her bills.*
  - Support: *I could help her do this or she could use a bookkeeping service.*

For Advisors

Use the above activity with an adult child client who is worried about their parents or an elderly loved one. Once the client has completed the activity, role-play the conversation with the person or couple. Have the client coach you on how he or she believes the parent will react to the inquiry. Then play out a best-case, worst-case, and most likely scenario. Next, have the client play the role of the parent, as this gives the client a chance to see how it might feel to be approached with these concerns. Again, role-play the best-case, worst-case, and most likely scenario. By helping your client practice this money talk, you are fostering trust and also setting the client up for success. These two things are sure to make you more referable.

Conclusion: It's Time for a Revolution

Be the change that you wish to see in the world.

—Mahatma Gandhi

Imagine a world where partners talk about money, resolve financial disagreements, and raise financially intelligent children. Women are paid equitably and are not penalized financially for their gender. In this society, parents are free to share their values, goals, and dreams with the next generation, and proactively plan and communicate their eldercare wishes to their children. In this world, financial advisors embrace the human side of finance and facilitate money communication between couples and families. In this society, money silence no longer exists.

I want to make this world a reality, but I need your help. I need you to join the *Breaking Money Silence* revolution. You can become a revolutionary in your family, your community, or in the financial services industry. Whatever action you take, it will be worth it as talking about money with those you love does enrich your life. Trust me, I know, as I am taking this journey with you. Yes, I started a while ago, but you can catch up. By now, you have read the book, completed the Money Talk Challenges, and have greater insight into your relationship with money than ever before. You just need to keep the ball rolling.

If you are an advisor, you are uniquely positioned to help couples and families shatter money taboos and talk more openly about finances. Doing so is good for your clients and your business. Facilitating wealth conversations is a unique, human skill, one that cannot be replaced by technology. When done well, this service can set you apart from the competition, attract over half of the population (also known as female clients), and provide a great avenue for connecting with the next generation of clients. It helps families successfully pass on wealth while you retain their business even when the power to make decisions shifts hands.

If we all band together, as partners, as parents, as family members, and as advisors, we can shatter money taboos and start openly and honestly talking about money in our society. Here are a few ideas on how you can act in revolutionary ways in your life.

Share This Book with a Friend

Social change happens when one person takes a risk to go against the grain. It is as if that one person is a droplet falling on a still pond. There is a ripple effect. You can be that droplet. Share this book with a friend, a family member, your financial advisor, or the local library. The more people who know about the high price they pay for money silence, and how to stop paying so much for it, the more effective this revolution will be.

Ask Your Advisor for Help

Let your financial advisor, banker, accountant, or lawyer know that you want help engaging in financial conversations with your partner, parents, children, or employer. Tell these professionals that you prefer to work with advisors who discuss both the technical and human side of finance with their clients, and that offering these services makes good business sense.

If you are a financial advisor, read, "A Call to Action for Financial Advisors" at http://breakingmoneysilence.com/advisor-call-to-action for tips on how you can lead the *Breaking Money Silence* revolution in your industry.

Keep the Conversation Going

Money talk is not a one-time event. It is a series of dialogues over your lifetime. When an opportunity arises to ask a curious question about another person's money mindset, money history, or financial perspective, dare to speak up. Be a role model for what healthy financial communication looks like, and demonstrate that the goal is progress not perfection. Dare to try, fail, learn, and grow with every conversation.

One of the best parts of writing a book is hearing about the impact it has had on those who read it. Let me know how these ideas resonate with you, and share your thoughts on how you creatively continue the revolution in your life and your community. Join the conversation and meet other revolutionaries by liking and following my Facebook page at https://www.facebook.com/kathleenburnskingsbury/. Reach out to me on Twitter at @KBKspeaks and use the hashtag #BreakingMoneySilence. Or e-mail me at info@breakingmoneysilence.com.

Let's keep the conversation going! I just know that together we can end money silence in society and in our lives for good.

—Kathleen

Resource Guide

Listed below are resources to help you break money silence in your personal and professional life. The books, online resources, and organizations are categorized by topic area, with each one providing valuable information for you and the advisors you work with.

Aging

Books

Learning to Speak Alzheimer's: A Groundbreaking Approach for Everyone Dealing with the Disease

By Joanne Koenig Coste

This book offers a practical approach to the emotional well-being of both patients and caregivers that emphasizes relating to patients in their own reality. It includes hundreds of tips, including how to cope with the diagnosis, how to adjust to the disease's progression, and how to help the patient talk about the illness.

The 36-Hour Day: A Family Guide to Caring for People Who Have Alzheimer Disease, Related Dementias, and Memory Loss

By Nancy L. Mace and Peter V. Rabins

Revised and updated, this guide features the latest information on the causes of dementia and how to manage the early stages of the disease. It also includes information on the prevention of dementia, and how to find appropriate living arrangements for the person who has this illness and can no longer live at home. A section on financial issues is included.

Organizations

Alzheimer's Association

http://www.alz.org

Founded in 1980, the Alzheimer's Association advances research to end Alzheimer's disease and dementia while enhancing care for those living with the disease. The website offers educational resources, financial and legal information, support group listings, and referrals to treatment facilities across the country.

National Adult Protective Services Association

http://www.napsa-now.org/

Formed in 1989, the goal is to provide a forum for sharing information, solving problems, and improving the quality of services for victims of elder abuse including neglect, abuse, and financial exploitation.

Coaching and Counseling

Credentialed Coach Finder

http://www.coachfederation.org/

This is a coaching referral service that is funded by the International Coaching Federation. You can search for coaches based on their credentials, services, and/or fee schedule.

Financial Therapy Association

https://www.financialtherapyassociation.org/

This organization offers referrals to financial therapy professionals who understand the psychology of money and work with individuals, couples, and families to improve their financial communication skills and their relationships with finances.

Therapist Locator

http://www.therapistlocator.net/

Therapist Locator is a public service of the American Association of Marriage and Family Therapy (AAMFT) Research and Education Foundation. It helps you search for a qualified marriage and family therapist in your area.

Emotional Intelligence

Books

Emotional Intelligence: Why It Can Matter More Than IQ

By Daniel Goleman

A classic work on emotional intelligence, this book is offers insight into your "two minds"—the rational and the emotional—and how they together shape your destiny.

Social Intelligence: The New Science of Human Relationships

By Daniel Goleman

In this book, the author shows you how your emotional intelligence impacts relationships with your friends, family members, and your coworkers.

Financial Advisors

Books

How to Give Financial Advice to Couples: Balancing High-Net-Worth Partners' Needs

By Kathleen Burns Kingsbury

Written as a follow-up to *How to Give Financial Advice to Women*, this book explains couples dynamics around money and offers tips and tools for advisors to be more couple-friendly in their client engagements.

How to Give Financial Advice to Women: Attracting and Retaining High-Net-Worth Female Clients

By Kathleen Burns Kingsbury

This practical book helps advisors understand the wants and needs of affluent female clients and shows them how to appeal to this group of loyal investors. First, it breaks down the psychological fundamentals of women and wealth, and then it outlines the skills professionals need to effectively communicate with and advise affluent women.

Working with the Emotional Investor: Financial Psychology for Wealth Managers

By Chris White with Richard Koonce

This book is an invaluable resource for wealth managers advising individuals, couples, and families. The book explains why human emotions drive all investors' behavior and makes a powerful case for why advisors need to be aware of such emotions in advising clients.

Organization

Purposeful Planning Institute

http://purposefulplanninginstitute.com/

A membership organization that offers advisors and related professionals (estate attorneys, family wealth consultants, psychologists, CPAs, etc.) who work with high-net-worth and ultra-high-net-worth clients education and training on a variety of issues, including working with nontraditional families and the psychology of money and wealth.

Legacy and Estate Planning

Books

Legacy Lifeprint

By Kathleen M. Rehl

https://purposefulplanninginstitute.com/legacy-lifeprint/

Use this free checklist to personalize the stories, values, wealth, and aspirations you would like to share with your family and future generations.

What if . . . Workbook

By Gwen Morgan

This is a unique, fill-in-the-blank organizational guide that leads you through the necessary steps for getting your affairs in order in one central location. It serves as a valuable resource for families to begin communication about issues that can be difficult to address.

Organization

The Conversation Project

http://theconversationproject.org/

The Conversation Project is dedicated to helping people talk about their wishes for end-of-life care. The project's organizers believe that it's time to transform our culture so we shift from not talking about dying to talking about it.

Financial Intelligence for the Next Generation

Books

Finance Is Personal: Making Your Money Work for You in College and Beyond

By Kim Stephenson and Ann B. Hutchins

This is a book for college-bound young adults on how to create a financial plan for going to school. It serves as a great introduction to the key elements of financial planning and how to start your adult life on a solid financial foundation.

Raising Financially Fit Kids

By Joline Godfrey

This book provides a developmental map for teaching children ages 5 to 18 how to master the 10 basic money skills. It includes creative activities for engaging young adults in learning about money and offers insight into what makes a young person become a financially responsible and secure adult.

Raised Healthy, Wealthy & Wise

By Coventry Edwards-Pitt

Raising children amid wealth presents some unique challenges. Nationally recognized wealth advisor Coventry Edwards-Pitt draws on her many years of professional experience to interview successful heirs and uncover what works—and what doesn't—in raising wealthy children to lead fulfilling and productive lives.

Organizations

Jumpstart Coalition for Personal Financial Literacy

http://www.jumpstart.org/

A coalition of diverse financial education stakeholders works to educate and prepare young people for life-long financial success, and offers conferences and trainings.

National Council on Economic Education

http://councilforeconed.org/

It prepares educators to teach personal finance and economics in the classroom by providing them with free professional development workshops, programs, and online resources.

Websites

Feed the Pig

http://www.feedthepig.com

A playful financial literacy website focused on helping you save more responsibly. Sign up for weekly reminders delivered to your e-mail address, including tips on how to save more and spend less.

SALT Money

http://www.saltmoney.org

Financial literacy website targeted for college students (from age 18 to 26). Topics include saving, spending, student loans, and negotiating salaries. Learning tools include games, quizzes, videos, and articles to make learning about finance fun and interactive.

Sammy Rabbit

http://sammyrabbit.com/

This website provides an array of simple and effective strategies for teaching children in first to third grade how to save. Tools include songs, videos, coloring books, and live performances.

Life Transitions

Books

Moving Forward on Your Own: A Financial Guidebook for Widows

By Kathleen M. Rehl

This practical workbook helps widows be more confident, knowledgeable, and secure about their money matters during this transition.

The New Love Deal: Everything You Must Know before Marrying, Moving In, or Moving On!

By Gemma Allen, Michele Lowrance, and Terry Savage

This book explores the financial and practical issues that couples confront, and the agreements that can resolve these differences before they destroy the relationship. This book helps you understand your legal and financial options.

Money Psychology

Books

Creating Wealth from the Inside Out Workbook

By Kathleen Burns Kingsbury

This workbook offers practical information and activities to help you change how you think and feel about money. Great for individuals and couples as it helps readers learn to identify and talk about their money mindsets.

The Financial Wisdom of Ebenezer Scrooge: 5 Principles to Transform Your Relationship with Money

By Ted Klontz, Rick Kahler, and Brad Klontz

This book teaches readers about money beliefs by using the character Scrooge from the Charles Dickens story *A Christmas Carol*. Tips and tools help readers gain insight into their money scripts, how these beliefs impact their financial habits, and how changing their thoughts about money can alter their financial health.

The Secret Language of Money: How to Make Smarter Financial Decisions and Live a Richer Life

By David Krueger with John David Mann

A classic in money psychology, this book offers you a guided tour to the subconscious meanings people give money, and the conflicted ways and reasons people tend to make the same money mistakes over and over. The book offers tips and techniques for how you can avoid these investor and financial errors in your own life.

Podcasts and Audio Recordings

Breaking Money Silence Podcast Series

By Kathleen Burns Kingsbury

http://www.breakingmoneysilence.com/podcast

A podcast series aimed at helping all of us talk more openly about money. Each 20-minute interview features a special guest and a money myth that they want to bust wide open.

Money Groundwork: Enriching Your Relationship with Money

By Shell Tain

http://shelltain.com/money-self-hypnosis/

Shell Tain and hypnotherapist Gary Meyer created this audio recording to help the listener reframe and change the beliefs that keep them from having a great relationship with money.

Personal Finances

Books

The Feel Rich Project

By Michael F. Kay

What does it mean to you to be rich? Find out by reflecting on your money history and experience and then develop a financial plan based on your own belief system. Use this book as a guide to help propel you into a whole new mindset regarding money and happiness.

The Mindful Money Mentality

By Holly P. Thomas

Written by a financial planner with over 25 years of experience, this is a personal finance book with a mindful twist. Readers learn how to understand their relationship with money and develop a spending plan based on their values.

On My Own Two Feet: A Modern Girl's Guide to Personal Finance

By Manisha Thakor and Sharon Kedar

Using their financial planning experience, the authors teach young women what they need to know about saving and investing, in user-friendly language.

Websites

LearnVest.com

http://www.LearnVest.com

The mission of this organization is to help people take control of their finances by increasing their financial literacy and helping them budget and plan for the future. LearnVest offers free services as well as low-cost expert advice to individuals to make better financial decisions.

Mint

https://www.mint.com/

Mint allows you to view all your financial data in one place. Using the website or the app, you can plan and track budgets, pay bills, and set financial goals. Mint also allows you to check your credit score and receive alerts about your accounts.

Philanthropy

Book

Inspired Philanthropy: Your Step-by-Step Guide to Creating a Giving Plan and Leaving a Legacy

By Tracy Gary

The newest edition of this classic book shows how anyone can align and integrate values, passions, and dreams for their communities and families into their giving and legacy plans. The book includes tips on how to make a difference by creating giving and legacy plans, what questions to ask nonprofits, and how to partner with advisors and nonprofit leaders for inspired outcomes.

Organization

Women's Philanthropy Institute

https://philanthropy.iupui.edu/institutes/womens-philanthropy-institute/

The Women's Philanthropy Institute (WPI) is part of the Lilly Family School of Philanthropy, Indiana University-Purdue University Indianapolis. The WPI helps us to better understand the powerful role of women leaders in 21st-century philanthropy, how to leverage that power, why gender matters in philanthropy, and works to facilitate a change in societal perceptions about who is philanthropic.

Retirement

Books

The Couple's Retirement Puzzle: 10 Must-Have Conversations for Creating an Amazing New Life Together

By Roberta Taylor and Dorian Mintzer

The most important asset you have during retirement often is your partner, yet many couples aren't sure where to begin to prepare for retired life or what to consider as they do. This book reveals 10 key conversations couples should tackle before retirement to ensure a rewarding second half of life together, including: if and when to retire, how to talk about money without fighting, and changing roles and identity.

Journal Your Way to Retirement

By Joan Gagnon

The first in a series of "Journal Your Way To" books written by an experienced financial planner. This book helps you identify what your heart and soul desire for this next phase of your life and offers a series of journaling exercises to assist you in the process.

Women's Empowerment

Books

Confidence Code

By Katty Kay and Claire Shipman

The interviews in this book, a blend of the experts' opinions and personal discoveries, are unique, enjoyable, and address the conversation on women and confidence in a very meaningful way for the reader.

Knowing Your Value: Women, Money, and Getting What You're Worth

By Mika Brzezinski

An in-depth look at how women today achieve their deserved recognition and financial worth. Through interviews with prominent women and men, Brzezinski reveals why women are paid less and the pitfalls women face when trying to get their worth at work while trying to move up in their field.

The Secrets of Six-Figure Women: Surprising Strategies to Up Your Earnings and Change Your Life

By Barbara Stanny

This book explores the traits financially successful women possess, and offers practical guidance to those women who aspire to increase their wealth.

Organization

Ellevate Professional Network

https://www.ellevatenetwork.com/

Professional businesswomen's organization that strives to empower women in the workplace and advance their corporate career by helping them connect, learn, and invest in themselves and others. Ellevate includes a professional network, live and online events, and resources on workplace diversity and inclusion.

Notes

Chapter 1. The Last Taboo: Money Talk

1. Wells Fargo. 2014. "Conversations about Personal Finance More Difficult than Religion and Politics, According to New Wells Fargo Survey." February 20. Accessed October 27, 2016. https://www.wellsfargo.com/about/press/2014/20140220_financial-health/.

2. Fidelity Investments. n.d. "2015 Couples Retirement Study Fact Sheet." Accessed October 26, 2016. https://www.fidelity.com/bin-public/060_www_fidelity_com/documents/couples-retirement-fact-sheet.pdf.

3. Tractman, Richard. 1999. "The Money Taboo: Its Effects in Everyday Life and in the Practice of Psychotherapy." *Clinical Social Work Journal* Vol. 27, No. 3, pp. 275–288.

4. Wells Fargo, "Conversations about Personal Finance."

5. Transferwise. 2016. "We Asked People from Different Countries What They Earned. You'll Never Guess What Happened." Accessed October 26, 2016. https://transferwise.com/us/blog/we-asked-people-from-different-countries-what-they-earned-youll-never-guess-what-happened.

6. Segal, Richard M. 2008. "Shirt Sleeves to Shirt Sleeves in Three Generations." *Corp!* July 1. Accessed October 24, 2016. https://www.corpmagazine.com/special-interests/family-business/shirt-sleeves-to-shirt-sleeves-in-three-generations/.

7. Tranquilli, Lou, interview by Kathleen Burns Kingsbury. 2016. *Personal Interview.* August 11.

8. McGrath, Maggie. 2015. "A Global Financial Literacy Test Finds That Just 57% of Adults in U.S. Are Financially Literate." *Forbes.* November 18. Accessed September 1, 2016. http://www.forbes.com/sites/maggiemcgrath/2015/11/18/in-a-global-test-of-financial-literacy-the-u-s/#d9339aa6a16f.

9. Money Matters on Campus. 2016. "Examining Financial Attitudes and Behaviors of Two-Year and Four-Year College Students." *Money Matters on Campus.* Accessed October 26, 2016. http://moneymattersoncampus.org/wp-content/uploads/2016/04/EverFi_WhitePaper_2016_FINAL-Web.pdf.

Chapter 2.   Silent but Deadly: The Cost of Staying Quiet

1. 2016. *World Gold Council*. Accessed March 24, 2016. http://www.gold.org/history-and-facts/gold-money.

2. TIAA-CREF. 2015. "Get Closer: Solving the Couples Conundrum." https://www.tiaa.org/public/pdf/Practice_Management+_Couples_Guidebook.pdf.

3. Charles Schwab. 2014. *Schwab Moneywise*. http://www.schwabmoneywise.com/public/moneywise/tools_resources/research.

4. Williams, Roy, and Vic Preisser. 2003. *Preparing Heirs: Five Steps to a Successful Transition of Family Wealth and Values*. San Francisco: Robert D. Reed.

5. American Psychological Association. n.d. *Stress in America: Paying with Our Health*. Accessed October 3, 2016. http://www.apa.org/news/press/releases/stress/2014/highlights.aspx.

6. CESI Debt Solutions. 2010. *National Survey Reveals the Truth about Marriage and Credit Cards*. Accessed October 15, 2016. https://www.cesisolutions.org/2013/09/national-survey-uncovers-new-information-sexually-transmitted-debt/.

7. Think Advisor. 2016. "How Advisors Can Stop Losing Clients' Heirs as Clients." *Think Advisor*. March 1. Accessed December 15, 2016. http://www.thinkadvisor.com/2016/03/01/how-advisors-can-stop-losing-clients-heirs-as-clie?slreturn=1482446232.

8. National Foundation for Credit Counseling. 2013. *National Foundation for Credit Counseling Survey*. May. Accessed October 15, 2016. https://www.nfcc.org/press/multimedia/news-releases/two-thirds-of-engaged-couples-express-negative-attitudes-toward-discussing-money/.

9. Dunham, Troy. 2014. "Money." *Love and Money*. June 1. http://time.com/money/2800576/love-money-by-the-numbers/.

10. Klontz, Brad: Klontz, Ted. 2009. *Mind Over Money*. New York: Broadway Books.

11. National Endowment for Financial Education (NEFE). 2016. *Two in Five Americans Confess to Financial Infidelity Against Their Partner*. February 11. Accessed October 1, 2016. http://www.nefe.org/press-room/news/americans-confess-to-financial-infidelity.aspx.

12. National Endowment for Financial Education (NEFE). 2016. *Two in Five Americans Confess to Financial Infidelity Against Their Partner*. February 11. Accessed October 1, 2016. http://www.nefe.org/press-room/news/americans-confess-to-financial-infidelity.aspx.

13. TD Bank. 2016. "TD Bank Surveys and Research." *TD Bank Love and Money Survey 2016*. July. Accessed September 30, 2016. https://mediaroom.tdbank.com/loveandmoney2016.

14. Hewlee, Sylvia A., Andrea T. Moffitt, and Melinda Marshall. 2014. "Harnessing the Power of the Purse:Female Investors and Global Opportunities for

Growth." *Talent Innovation.* Accessed October 16, 2016. http://www.talentin novation.org/assets/HarnessingThePowerOfThePurse_ExecSumm-CTI-CONFI DENTIAL.pdf.

15. Prudential Financial. 2015. *Financial Experience & Behaviors Among Women.* Accessed 2016. http://corporate.prudential.com/media/managed/wm/ WM-womens-research-summary.html.

16. AAUW. 2016. "79 Examples of How Women Are Still Treated Unequally."

17. *Women & Wealth Magazine.* 2016. "Bridging the Funding Gap." 13.

18. AAUW. 2016. "79 Examples of How Women Are Still Treated Unequally."

19. Bose, Shubhomita. 2016. "Women Owned Business Sees 12 Percent Rise in Revenue, Says Biz2Credit." *Small Business Trends.* March 4. Accessed October 20, 2016. https://smallbiztrends.com/2016/03/2016-women-owned-business-study-biz2credit.html.

20. Leibbrandt, Andreas, and John A. List. 2012. "Do Women Avoid Salary Negotiations? Evidence from a Large Scale Natural Field Experiment." *National Bureau of Ecomonomic Research* 1–26.

21. Robbins, Christopher. 2016. "Americans Prefer 'Sex Talk' with Kids over 'Aging Talk' with Parents." *Financial Advisor.* July 6. Accessed September 30, 2016. http://www.fa-mag.com/news/americans-prefer-the—sex-talk—with-kids-to-the—aging-talk-with-parents-27848.html.

22. McVicker, Barbara. n.d. *Barbara McVicker.* Accessed September 24, 2016. http://www.barbaramcvicker.com/.

23. Alzheimer's Association. n.d. http://www.alz.org/facts/overivew.asp.

24. Alzheimer's Association. 2014. *2014 Alzheimer's Disease Facts and Figures.* March. https://www.ncbi.nlm.nih.gov/pubmed/24818261.

25. Alzheimer's Association. 2014. *2014 Alzheimer's Disease Facts and Figures.* March. https://www.ncbi.nlm.nih.gov/pubmed/24818261.

26. McVicker, Barbara. n.d. *Barbara McVicker.* Accessed September 24, 2016. http://www.barbaramcvicker.com/.

27. American Express. n.d. "Consortium for Research on Emotional Intelligence in Organization." *Emotional Competence Training Program.* Accessed October 16, 2016. http://www.eiconsortium.org/pdf/emotional_competence_training.pdf.

28. Silbernagel, Jim, interview by Kathleen Burns Kingsbury. 2016. *Personal Interview* (May 31).

29. Silbernagel, Jim, interview by Kathleen Burns Kingsbury. 2016. *Personal Interview* (May 31).

30. Trachtman, Richard. 1999. "The Money Taboo: Its Effects in Everyday Life and in the Practice of Psychotherapy." *Clinical Social Work Journal* Vol. 27, No. 3, pp. 275–288.

31. Britt, Sonya L., Bradley T. Klontz, Racquel Tibbetts, and Linda Leitz. 2015. "The Financial Health of Mental Health Professionals." *Journal of Financial Therapy* Vol. 6, No. 1, pp. 17–32.

Chapter 3. All Men Are Financially Literate and Other Myths about Gender and Money

1. Hewlee, Sylvia A., Andrea T. Moffitt, and Melinda Marshall. 2014. "Harnessing the Power of the Purse: Female Investors and Global Opportunities for Growth." *Talent Innovation*. Accessed October 16, 2016. http://www.talentinno vation.org/assets/HarnessingThePowerOfThePurse_ExecSumm-CTI-CONFI DENTIAL.pdf.

2. CFP Board. 2016. "CFP Board's Women's Initiative (WIN)." *CFP Board*. http://www.cfp.net/about-cfp-board/cfp-board's-women-s-initiative-(win).

3. Fidelity Investments. 2015. "Money Fit Women Study." *Fidelity*. Accessed 2016. https://www.fidelity.com/bin-public/060_www_fidelity_com/documents/ women-fit-money-study.pdf.

4. Barber, Brad M., and Terrance Odean. 2001. "Boys Will Be Boys: Gender, Overconfidence and Common Stock Investment." *The Quarterly Journal of Economics* 261–292. https://faculty.haas.berkeley.edu/odean/papers/gender/BoysWill BeBoys.pdf.

5. Fidelity Investments. 2015. "Money Fit Women Study." *Fidelity*. Accessed 2016. https://www.fidelity.com/bin-public/060_www_fidelity_com/documents/ women-fit-money-study.pdf.

6. Beckton, Clare, Samina M. Saifuddin, Janice McDonald, and Umut R. Ozkan. n.d. "A Force to Reckon with: Women, Entrepreneuship and Risk." *Carleton University*. https://carleton.ca/cwppl/wp-content/uploads/A_Force_To_Reckon_ With_BN.pdf.

7. Bose, Shubhomita. 2016. "Women Owned Business Sees 12 Percent Rise in Revenue, Says Biz2Credit." *Small Business Trends*. March 4. Accessed October 20, 2016. https://smallbiztrends.com/2016/03/2016-women-owned-busi ness-study-biz2credit.html.

8. Teare, Gene, and Ned Desmond. 2016. "The First Comprehensive Study on Women in Venture Capital and Their Impact on Female Founders." *Techcrunch*. April 19. Accessed December 12, 2016. https://techcrunch. com/2016/04/19/the-first-comprehensive-study-on-women-in-venture-capital/.

9. Allianz Life Insurance Company of North America. 2008. "New Allianz 'Women, Money and Power' Study." *Allianz*. June 24. Accessed 2016. https:// www.allianz.com/en/press/news/studies/news_2008-06-24-1.html/.

10. Barber, Brad M., and Terrance Odean. 2001. "Boys Will Be Boys: Gender, Overconfidence and Common Stock Investment." *The Quarterly Journal of Economics* Vol. 116, pp. 261–292. https://faculty.haas.berkeley.edu/odean/papers/ gender/BoysWillBeBoys.pdf.

11. Pew Research Center. 2014. "Millenials in Adulthood." *Pew Research Center*. March 7. Accessed December 9, 2016. http://www.pewsocialtrends.org/2014/ 03/07/millennials-in-adulthood/.

12. MacNeal, Caitlin. 2014. "GOP Lawmaker: Women Get Paid Less Because 'Men Are More Motivated'." *TPM*. April 24. Accessed February 16, 2017. http://

talkingpointsmemo.com/livewire/gop-lawmaker-women-paid-less-men-moti
vated.

13. Hartmann, Heidi, Jeffrey Hayes, and Jennifer Clark. 2014. "How Equal
Pay for Working Women Would Reduce Poverty and Grow the American Economy." *Institute forWomen's Policy Research*. January. http://www.iwpr.org/publica-
tions/pubs/how-equal-pay-for-working-women-would-reduce-poverty-and-
grow-the-american-economy.

14. Byham, Tacy. 2016. "#LeadLikeAGirl: How Can Women Leaders Ignite
Impact?. " *DDI*. February. Accessed November 1, 2016. http://www.ddiworld.
com/blog/tmi/february-2016/leadlikeagirl-how-can-women-leaders-ignite-
impact.

15. CFP Board. 2016. "CFP Board's Women's Initiative (WIN)." *CFP Board*.
http://www.cfp.net/about-cfp-board/cfp-board's-women-s-initiative-(win).

Chapter 4. It Is Not about the Price of Milk

1. Prudential. 2014. "The Hispanic American Financial Experience." Prudential. Accessed December 29, 2016. https://www.prudential.com/media/man-
aged/hispanic_bn/prudential_hafe_researchstudy_2014_bn.pdf.

2. Prudential. 2016. "Asian Ameriican Financial Experience." *Prudential*.
Accessed December 29, 2016. https://www.prudential.com/documents/corp/
AsianAmerFinExperReport.pdf.

3. Dorsainvil, Rianka, interview by Kathleen Burns Kingsbury. 2016. *Personal Interview* (October 26).

4. T. Rowe Price. 2016. "Talking to Kids about Money Matters." *Money Confident Kids*. Accessed November 30, 2016. http://moneyconfidentkids.com/content/
money-confident-kids/en/us/parents/talking-to-kids-about-money-matters.html.

5. Stephenson, Kim, and Ann B. Hutchins. 2015. *Finance Is Personal: Making
Your Own Money Work for You in College and Beyond*. Santa Barbara, CA:
ABC-CLIO.

6. Taylor, Chris. 2015. "What Buddhism Can Teach Us about Money."
Money. August 25. Accessed December 1, 2016. http://time.com/money/4009735/
buddhism-money-lessons/.

7. Klontz, Brad, and Ted Klontz. 2009. *Mind Over Money*. New York: Broadway Books.

8. Klontz, Brad T., Paul Sullivan, Martin C. Seay, and Anthony Canale. 2015.
"The Wealthy: A Financial Psychological Profile." *Consulting Psychology Journal:
Practice and Research* 67 (2): 127–143.

Chapter 5. The Buck Stops Here: Dare to Break the Silence

1. Shikany, Kelly, interview by Kathleen Burns Kingsbury. 2017. *Personal
Interview* (February 17).

2. Encylopaedia Britannica. 2009. "Marquess of Queensberry Rules." *Encylopaedia Britannica*. Accessed December 28, 2016. https://www.britannica.com/sports/Marquess-of-Queensberry-rules.

3. Kingsbury, Kathleen Burns. 2013. *How to Give Financial Advice to Couples*. McGraw-Hill.

4. Rehl, Kathleen, interview by Kathleen Burns Kingsbury. 2016. *Personal Interview* (November 08).

5. n.d. *Serena Williams*. Accessed January 1, 2017. http://serenawilliams.com/trophy-case/.

6. Tain, Shell, interview by Kathleen Burns Kingsbury. 2017. *Personal Interview* (February 17).

Chapter 6. Curiosity Killed the Cat but Saved the Conversation

1. Fidelity. 2015. "2015 Couples Retirement Study Fact Sheet." *Fidelity*. https://www.fidelity.com/bin-public/060_www_fidelity_com/documents/couples-retirement-fact-sheet.pdf.

2. Tranquilli, Lou, interview by Kathleen Burns Kingsbury. 2017. *Personal Interview* (February 17).

3. Skikany, Kelly, interview by Kathleen Burns Kingsbury. 2017. *Personal Interview* (February 17).

Chapter 7. Until Death (or Divorce) Do You Part: Difficult Couple Money Conversations

1. Deccan Chronicle. 2016. "5 Ways Money Wrecks a Relationship." *Deccan Chronicle*. September 27. http://www.deccanchronicle.com/lifestyle/sex-and-relationship/270916/5-ways-money-wrecks-a-relationship.html.

2. TD Bank. 2016. "TD Bank Surveys and Research." *TD Bank Love and Money Survey 2016*. July. Accessed September 30, 2016. https://mediaroom.tdbank.com/loveandmoney2016.

3. TD Bank. 2016. "TD Bank Surveys and Research." *TD Bank Love and Money Survey 2016*. July. Accessed September 30, 2016. https://mediaroom.tdbank.com/loveandmoney2016.

4. Desilver, Drew. 2014. "5 Facts about Love and Marriage." *Pew Research Center*. February 14. http://www.pewresearch.org/fact-tank/2014/02/14/5-facts-about-love-and-marriage/.

5. Desilver, Drew. 2014. "5 Facts about Love and Marriage." *Pew Research Center*. February 14. http://www.pewresearch.org/fact-tank/2014/02/14/5-facts-about-love-and-marriage/.

6. TD Bank. 2016. "TD Bank Surveys and Research." *TD Bank Love and Money Survey 2016*. July. Accessed September 30, 2016. https://mediaroom.tdbank.com/loveandmoney2016.

7. Slater, Suzanne, interview by Kathleen Burns Kingsbury. 2017. *Personal Interview* (February 3).

8. Sexton, James J. 2016. "How to Prepare for that Prenup Conversation." *The Huffington Post*. February 26. http://www.huffingtonpost.com/james-j-sexton-/how-to-prepare-for-that-prenup-conversation_b_9319618.html.

9. Banschick, Mark. 2012. "The High Failure Rate of Second and Third Marriages." *Psychology Today*. February 6. Accessed February 4, 2017. https://www.psychologytoday.com/blog/the-intelligent-divorce/201202/the-high-failure-rate-second-and-third-marriages.

10. Roberts, Sam. 2013. "Divorce After 50 Grows More Common." *The New York Times*. September 20. Accessed February 4, 2017. http://www.nytimes.com/2013/09/22/fashion/weddings/divorce-after-50-grows-more-common.html.

11. Everplans. 2015. "Everplans Research Shows Consumers Want to Plan for Future, but Have Difficulty Getting Started." *PR Newswire*. September 16. Accessed February 1, 2017. http://www.prnewswire.com/news-releases/everplans-research-shows-consumers-want-to-plan-for-future-but-have-difficulty-getting-started-300143928.html.

12. Joffe-Walt, Chana. 2014. "The Town Where Everyone Talks about Death." *NPR*. March 4. Accessed February 1, 2017. http://www.npr.org/sections/money/2014/03/05/286126451/living-wills-are-the-talk-of-the-town-in-la-crosse-wis.

13. Joffe-Walt, Chana. 2014. "The Town Where Everyone Talks about Death." *NPR*. March 4. Accessed February 1, 2017. http://www.npr.org/sections/money/2014/03/05/286126451/living-wills-are-the-talk-of-the-town-in-la-crosse-wis.

14. Morgan, Gwen, interview by Kathleen Burns Kingsbury. 2017. *Personal Interview* (February 16).

Chapter 8. Kids and Money Talk: Raising a Financially Intelligent Next Generation

1. Council for Economic Education. 2016. "Survey of the States: Economic and Personal Finance Education in Our Nation's Schools 2016." *Cocuil for Economic Education*. Accessed January 29, 2017. http://councilforeconed.org/wp/wp-content/uploads/2016/02/sos-16-final.pdf.

2. Shape America. 2016. "Shape of the Nation." *Shape America*. Accessed January 29, 2017. http://www.shapeamerica.org/advocacy/son/2016/upload/Shape-of-the-Nation-2016_web.pdf.

3. U.S. Bank. (2015, July 7). 2015 U.S. Bank Students and Personal Finance Study. Retrieved from https://financialgenius.usbank.com/dam/documents/pdf/U.S._Bank_Students_and_Personal_Finance_Study.pdf.

4. U.S. Bank. (2015, July 7). *2015 U.S. Bank Students and Personal Finance Study*. Retrieved from https://financialgenius.usbank.com/dam/documents/pdf/U.S._Bank_Students_and_Personal_Finance_Study.pdf.

5. U.S. Bank. (2015, July 7). *2015 U.S. Bank Students and Personal Finance Study.* Retrieved from https://financialgenius.usbank.com/dam/documents/pdf/ U.S._Bank_Students_and_Personal_Finance_Study.pdf

6. Cnossen, Joan, interview by Kathleen Burns Kingsbury. 2017. *Personal Interview* (January 18).

7. T. Rowe Price. 2016. "8th Annual Parents, Kids, and Money Survey." *T. Rowe Price.* Accessed January 22, 2017. https://corporate.troweprice.com/Money-Confident-Kids/images/emk/2016pkmresultsdeckfinal-160322181149.pdf.

8. T. Rowe Price. 2016. "8th Annual Parents, Kids, and Money Survey." *T. Rowe Price.* Accessed January 22, 2017. https://corporate.troweprice.com/Money-Confident-Kids/images/emk/2016pkmresultsdeckfinal-160322181149.pdf.

9. T. Rowe Price. 2016. "8th Annual Parents, Kids, and Money Survey." *T. Rowe Price.* Accessed January 22, 2017. https://corporate.troweprice.com/Money-Confident-Kids/images/emk/2016pkmresultsdeckfinal-160322181149.pdf.

10. T. Rowe Price. 2016. "8th Annual Parents, Kids, and Money Survey." *T. Rowe Price.* Accessed January 22, 2017. https://corporate.troweprice.com/Money-Confident-Kids/images/emk/2016pkmresultsdeckfinal-160322181149.pdf.

11. T. Rowe Price. 2016. "8th Annual Parents, Kids, and Money Survey." *T. Rowe Price.* Accessed January 22, 2017. https://corporate.troweprice.com/Money-Confident-Kids/images/emk/2016pkmresultsdeckfinal-160322181149.pdf.

12. T. Rowe Price. 2016. "8th Annual Parents, Kids, and Money Survey." *T. Rowe Price.* Accessed January 22, 2017. https://corporate.troweprice.com/Money-Confident-Kids/images/emk/2016pkmresultsdeckfinal-160322181149.pdf.

13. Campaign for a Commercial-Free Childhood. n.d. "Marketing to Children Overview." Commercial Free Childhood. Accessed January 22, 2017. http://www.commercialfreechildhood.org/sites/default/files/overview.pdf.

14. Campaign for a Commercial-Free Childhood. n.d. "Marketing to Children Overview." Commercial Free Childhood. Accessed January 22, 2017. http://www.commercialfreechildhood.org/sites/default/files/overview.pdf.

15. Kelman, Jessica. 2016. "Is There a TV in Your Child's Room?" *Great Schools.* October 28. Accessed January 29, 2017. http://www.greatschools.org/gk/articles/effects-of-tv-in-children-bedroom/.

16. Moses, Lucia. 2014. "A Look at Kids' Exposure to Ads." *Adweek.* March 11. Accessed January 29, 2017. http://www.adweek.com/digital/look-kids-exposure-ads-156191/.

17. Campaign for a Commercial-Free Childhood. n.d. "Marketing to Children Overview." Commercial Free Childhood. Accessed January 22, 2017. http://www.commercialfreechildhood.org/sites/default/files/overview.pdf.

18. Renick, Sam, interview by Kathleen Burns Kingsbury. 2017. *Personal Interview* (January 6).

19. Renick, Sam, interview by Kathleen Burns Kingsbury. 2017. *Personal Interview* (January 6).

20. Renick, Sam, interview by Kathleen Burns Kingsbury. 2017. *Personal Interview* (January 6).

21. Godfrey, Joline. 2013. *Raising Financially Fit Kids.* New York, NY: Ten Speed Press.

Chapter 9. Raising Financially Fit Parents

1. Rosenblatt, Carolyn. 2013. "4 Financial Issues You Need to Discuss with Aging Parents." *Forbes.* August 19. Accessed January 30, 2017. http://www.forbes.com/sites/carolynrosenblatt/2013/08/19/smart-ways-to-talk-to-aging-parents-about-finances/#7da1c65a2853.

2. Robbins, Christopher. 2016. "Americans Prefer 'Sex Talk' with Kids over 'Aging Talk' with Parents." *Financial Advisor.* July 6. Accessed September 30, 2016. http://www.fa-mag.com/news/americans-prefer-the—sex-talk—with-kids-to-the—aging-talk-with-parents-27848.html.

3. Robbins, Christopher. 2016. "Americans Prefer 'Sex Talk' with Kids over 'Aging Talk' with Parents." *Financial Advisor.* July 6. Accessed September 30, 2016. http://www.fa-mag.com/news/americans-prefer-the—sex-talk—with-kids-to-the—aging-talk-with-parents-27848.html.

4. Alzheimer's Association. 2017. *Alzheimer's Association.* Accessed January 26, 2017. http://www.alz.org/.

5. Alzheimer's Association. 2014. *2014 Alzheimer's disease facts and figures.* March. https://www.ncbi.nlm.nih.gov/pubmed/24818261.

6. Clifford, Zachery, interview by Kathleen Burns Kingsbury. 2017. *Personal Interview* (January 28).

7. Bahramour, Tara. 2016. "Promise You'll Never Put Me in a Nursing Home." *The Washington Post.* February 25. Accessed January 30, 2017. https://www.washingtonpost.com/local/social-issues/promise-youll-never-put-me-in-a-nursing-home/2016/02/08/1ce8737c-cb62–11e5-a7b2–5a2f824b02c9_story.html?utm_term=.5b0ce0370d87.

8. Pelisser, Kelly, interview by Kathleen Burns Kingsbury. 2017. *Personal Interview* (January 17).

9. Pelisser, Kelly, interview by Kathleen Burns Kingsbury. 2017. *Personal Interview* (January 17).

10. Pelisser, Kelly, interview by Kathleen Burns Kingsbury. 2017. *Personal Interview* (January 17).

11. Norris, Joe, interview by Kathleen Burns Kingsbury. 2016. *Personal Interview* (August 10).

12. Norris, Joe, interview by Kathleen Burns Kingsbury. 2016. *Personal Interview* (August 10).

13. Tattersfield, Nikki, interview by Kathleen Burns Kingsbury. 2017. *Personal Interview* (September 19).

14. Tattersfield, Nikki, interview by Kathleen Burns Kingsbury. 2017. *Personal Interview* (September 19).

Index

Note: Page numbers *in italics* refer to figures and tables.

Williams, Serena, 85–86
Wills, 124, 125
Women: buying decisions, 20; female money mindset, 54; money and, 20–22; myths about wealth, 32–38; pay equity, 16, 20–22. *See also gender topics*

Women-owned businesses, 37
Women's Initiative Network, 43
Work ethic, 52

"You know better" mentality, 98–99

Zen Buddhism, 93

About the Author

Kathleen Burns Kingsbury is a wealth psychology expert, founder of KBK Wealth Connection, host of the *Breaking Money Silence* podcast, and an internationally published author. Her previous books include *Creating Wealth from the Inside Out Workbook*, *How to Give Financial Advice to Women,* and *How to Give Financial Advice to Couples.*

Kathleen is a sought-after keynote speaker and consultant on the topics of women and wealth and couples and money. Her mission is to empower women, couples, families, and their financial services providers to shatter money taboos and communicate more effectively about finances.

Photo by Gretje Ferguson

As an expert on financial psychology, Kathleen has been quoted in publications such as *The Wall Street Journal, The New York Times, Money Magazine, Today's Money,* and Forbes' *ForbesWoman.* Her articles have appeared in *American Banker Magazine,* CNBC.com, *Investment News, Investments & Wealth Monitor,* and other trade and consumer publications.

Kathleen is an adjunct lecturer at the McCallum Graduate School of Business at Bentley University, where she teaches psychology in financial planning. She received an undergraduate degree in finance from

Providence College and started her career in retail banking before becoming a commissioned bank examiner with the FDIC.

Due to her desire to coach executive management on improving performance, she attained a master's degree in psychology, became a Certified Professional Co-Active Coach (CPCC), and founded her consulting firm, KBK Wealth Connection.

When she is not working, Kathleen is an avid alpine skier who lives for the next powder day. In the off-season, she enjoys road and mountain biking, kayaking, and sailing. She lives with her husband and her cat, Avery, in the Mad River Valley of Vermont.

For more information, visit http://breakingmoneysilence.com.